Ida
From Abroad

*The timeless writings
of Ida B. Wells
from England in 1894*

All the best!

Michelle Duster

From Abroad

*The timeless writings
of Ida B. Wells
from England in 1894*

Compiled and Written
by Michelle Duster

Foreword by Troy Duster, Ph.D.

BENJAMIN WILLIAMS PUBLISHING
WWW.BWPUBLISHING.COM

Ida From Abroad

IDA FROM ABROAD
The timeless writings of Ida B. Wells from England in 1894

ISBN: 978-0-9802398-9-8
Printed in The United States of America

Benjamin Williams Publishing
500 N. Michigan Ave., Suite 300
Chicago, Illinois 60611
www.bwpublishing.com

In memory of
Alfreda Marguerita Barnett Duster
and
Ida Bell Barnett

CONTENTS

TWO WEAPONS IN ONE HAND

BY TROY DUSTER Ph.D.

etween mid-March and early July of 1894, the American anti-lynching crusader Ida B. Wells delivered 102 lectures to churches, clubs, boardrooms and civic councils all over Great Britain. She had a searing purpose to serve, and two weapons in her hand. She would wield them with impressive political skill, and in turn these would yield notable political success to her cause.

There are different phases or stages in the attempt to mobilize for social change. The first phase is one in which the advocates of change try to persuade, to exhort, to cajole, to explain, to reason, to plead – to, in short – deploy a wide variety of devices attempting to influence behavior by non-coercive means. A good example is the Temperance Movement. At its beginnings, this movement started off by trying to educate the population about the many problems of alcohol use and abuse. The early phases of Temperance saw women pleading with men, for their own good health and well-being, to stop drinking! These women used

1

pamphlets and leaflets, Sunday school instruction and Sunday church sermons, lectures at union halls, community town hall meetings – all with the purpose of trying to persuade, to influence behavior. Joseph Gusfield (1980) shows how, when this failed to move the country, the movement shifted to direct legal maneuvers – the passage of "dry laws" to forbid the sale of alcohol in select jurisdictions, accompanied by the now humorous Lysistrata parallel pledge of "lips that touch wine will never touch mine!" Of course we all know now that the coercive strategy would ultimately end in the passage of the 18th amendment to the U.S. Constitution in 1919 – and the more than decade-long experiment with alcohol Prohibition.

In different forms, this story is repeated through the history of social movements. The original "arguments" against slavery, for example, were exactly that: arguments. The abolitionists did not begin by advocating slave revolts or constitutional amendments, and certainly not a civil war. Instead, they tried to reason with their adversaries – they tried to use moral persuasion and exhortation to religious principles, at least at the start of the movement. And as with the later development with Prohibition, when persuasion and advocacy failed, there was the inexorable segue into law (the 1820 Missouri Compromise, which would prohibit slavery in new states) then ultimately to direct action – the extreme being John Brown's famous attempt of an armed slave uprising at Harper's Ferry.

And so it would be with the anti-lynching crusade of Ida B. Wells. She began with the firm belief that logic, reason and moral persuasion would prevail – that the simple acts of shining the light of truth on the

matter of lynching would turn the tide. This is some-
times called the phase of idealism – and it is almost
universal. Using her newspaper as a vehicle for illu-
minating the problem of lynching and other injustices
visited upon Blacks, in this early stage Wells believed
that whites of good faith would recognize the injustices once shown to them. Yet something in her own
experience had shaken her belief in the power of good
faith alone. Wells had literally gone on a journey from
idealism to a very different place. After the infamous
train ride in 1884 where she was refused the right to sit
in the ladies' coach – she sued, and won (she thought).
But the state Supreme Court overturned her victory,
thereby setting her along a pathway to another course
of action in the pursuit of racial equality.

Her disillusionment with the law as an instrument
was profound, but as Lincoln Steffens noted, disillusion is not a bad thing. Steffens saw "dis" illusion as
a necessary development -- that disillusion meant that
people no longer had illusions, and could thus get a
clearer picture of the realities facing them. Ida B. Wells'
disillusion from that experience would help transform
her into a clear-eyed realist assessing the nature of the
barriers in her path – and thus generating a burgeoning set of strategies to deal with those barriers.

At first, she advocated direct economic action in
the form of asking Blacks to boycott white businesses. While somewhat effective, boycotts are difficult to
sustain. Next, she advocated a mass exodus of Blacks
to the new territories opening up to the West. Again,
somewhat effective, but not all, most, or even many
had the wherewithal to make such a dramatic move.
Thus she came to a two-part strategy, each inter-locked

with the other, that would become very effective. What were those twined weapons?

The first part was the use of "shame." Anthropologists have long documented how shame is one of the most effective mechanisms of social control. Of course the vital ingredient is the assessment of which parties are the relevant ones (the strategic audience) for the shaming. This is where we begin to see Wells' strategic brilliance. She understood that "shame" would not work on audiences of whites if the weapon was confined inside the nation's borders. First, American newspapers owned by whites had already demonstrated a reluctance, even refusal to cover and publish stories about the horrors of lynching. The Tilden-Hayes compromise had pulled northern troops out of the South, abandoning the fate of the region to white supremacists. For the federal government to authorize a return to "interfere" with rights of southern states to police their own population would be an embarrassing admission of guilt for having refused to address gross injustices (a direct consequence of the troop withdrawal) at the end of Reconstruction.

Second, countries outside the United States had little interest in "covering up" reports of lawlessness in America. At the end of the 19th century, Great Britain still ruled a vast empire and wielded considerable economic and political power around the globe. If British public opinion could be brought around to see that their industrial machinery was implicated in supporting barbaric practices (think of the world-wide boycott of the apartheid regime in South Africa during the last quarter of the 20th century), then that would have an impact on the political will of southern agricultural-political elite. There was both heavy trade between England and the United States, a former break-away colony. British public opinion was still important to a significant portion of U.S. cultural, economic, and political elites. Ida B. Wells would learn to brilliantly exploit each of these vital connections with political acumen, playing on the fact that the American South was a significant exporter of raw cotton to the industrial mills of the United Kingdom. Cotton farmers would be highly sensitive to any hint of a boycott of their product.

Thus, Wells saw that a victory with shifting public opinion in Britain would join two powerful weapons: 1) shaming of the U.S. economic and cultural elite who would be stung by their British counterparts as ignoring the brutal and savage barbarism of lynching parties, and 2) the linked threat of a boycott of cotton.

American politicians had eagerly portrayed the U.S. as a reliable trade partner with little social or political strife. They had collectively decided to squash or at least quell the debate over lynching and its lawlessness – or at least to diminish, trivialize or ignore lynching as a significant problem. Wells' campaign was an immediate threat to these interests because it spread vivid accounts of horrific crimes against Blacks, most especially to an audience of potential allies and sympathizers in Great Britain. England had experienced its own internal fight revolving around financing the slave trade in the early 19th century, and their internecine wrenching debates were still fresh enough in the cultural memory (Hochschild 2005). Frederick Douglass had lived in England during the late 1840s, was a well-known figure, even revered by the strong

Christian abolitionist figures still very much a force in British politics. Thus, they would provide vital contacts, and would permit an orator as skilled as Wells a pre-tilled and fertile soil in which to deliver her message.

A measure of her success is that a new abolition society formed in London – generating donations to her cause. Her campaign in England, where she delivered over one hundred lectures mainly in the major cities, would change how the British viewed Americans, especially whites, as a result of the coverage that was given in the mainstream press. Just a few months after her return to the United States, Wells could be largely credited for the decision by the London Anti-Lynching Committee to come to America to investigate lynching. It was in this context that Virginia Governor Charles O'Ferrall – who had previously been highly critical of Wells for what he called her "slanders of the people and civil authorities of the South" – would "come around" to finally condemn lynching. He would boast, with the English visitors in earshot, that he had called out the state militia to protect Blacks who had been charged with "outraging a white woman." (Giddings 2008:324).

> Despite its own unsympathetic view of the British fact-finders, the *New York Times* predicted that "a good deal of interest will be awakened" when the committee's report was published.
> (Giddings 2008:325)

Even long-time adversaries such as Frances Willard would finally "come around" to renouncing the complicity of southern elites in the toleration of lynching

– grudgingly acknowledging that Wells had been right all along in her analysis. The on-going battles and enmity between Willard and Wells would persist, but the tug-of-war tilting towards anti-lynching would shift in Wells' direction, a direct result of her British tour strategy. So perhaps it is appropriate to end this introduction with the poem, written by Katherine Davis Tillman in the 1890s:

> *…Go on, thou brave woman leader,*
> *Spread our wrongs from shore unto shore,*
> *Until clothed with his rights is the Negro,*
> *And lynchings are no more …*
> *And the wise Afro-American mother,*
> *Who her children of heroine tells,*
> *Shall speak in tones of gratitude,*
> *The name of Ida B. Wells!*

THE
DAILY INTER OCEAN
NEWSPAPER ARTICLES

BY IDA B. WELLS FROM ENGLAND IN 1894

About the Articles

My grandmother, Alfreda M. Duster, donated her mother's (Ida B. Wells) work to the Regenstein Library at the University of Chicago (her alma mater) because she knew that the documents would be well preserved. However, some of her other articles are located in other archives such as The Chicago History Museum. Unfortunately, some of Ida's original work was lost due to fires or vandalism, so I was only able to work with the documents that could be archived and kept in reasonable condition.

Some of the original newspapers that are in the archives were torn and therefore challenging to read. What is included in this book is my best attempt to reproduce these articles and correspondences as close to the originals as possible.

My hope is that this book will make it easier for

those who are interested in and inspired by the writings of Ida B. Wells to have access to her work. Although this book reproduces her articles, the original newspaper pages are very interesting to see in their entirety. The pages include advertisements for a variety of items such as china, baking powder, bicycles, furniture, blood purifiers, and "female regulators." There are also building permits, engagement, wedding and death announcements, plus classified advertisements for apartment rentals for $15 - $25. Seeing this type of information gives one a more clear idea of how life was in Chicago in 1894.

Note About the Text

The spellings of some of the words included in these newspaper articles are different than how they're spelled today. In addition, there are some inconsistencies in spelling of words and names as well as a few typos in the original articles. With few exceptions, I decided to reproduce them exactly as they were originally written and printed.

Ida B. Wells used question marks and dashes in her writings to emphasize her opinion. The question marks that appear in the middle of sentences, enclosed in parentheses, are exactly as they appeared in the original articles.

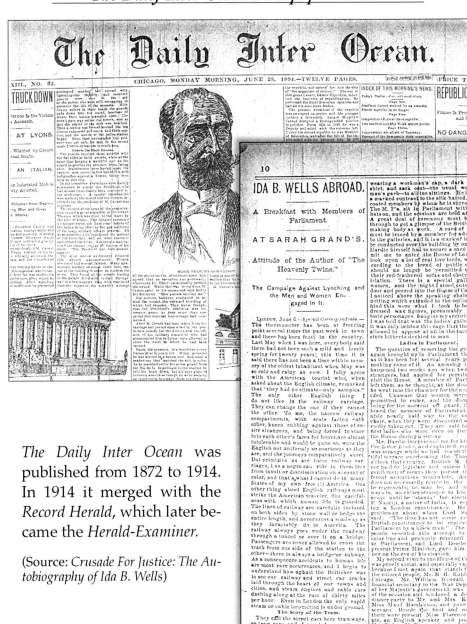

The Daily Inter Ocean was published from 1872 to 1914. In 1914 it merged with the *Record Herald*, which later became the *Herald-Examiner*.

(Source: *Crusade For Justice: The Autobiography of Ida B. Wells*)

11

IDA B. WELLS ABROAD.

The Nemesis of Southern Lynchers Again in England.

WELCOME TO LIVERPOOL.

Why She Was Invited to Pembroke Chapel.

An English Clergyman's Recollection of What He
Heard at the World's Fair.

LIVERPOOL, England, March 12* – *Special Corre-spondence.* – Directly after the burning alive of Henry Smith, at Paris, Texas, February, 1893; the writer received a letter inviting her to visit England and enlighten the natives on the lynching mania which seemed to prevail in the States. Needless to say I accepted the invitation with alacrity and within five days of its receipt sailed from New York. Ever since the suppression of my newspaper, the *Free Speech*, in Memphis, Tenn., in May, 1892, I had made unsuccessful attempts to be heard in the journals and on the platforms of the American people against lynching, which was fast becoming a national evil. When the way was opened in Great Britain I accepted gladly. Beginning in Aberdeen, Scotland, a tour was made throughout the largest cities of Scotland and England, and in each of these cities was established a "Society for the Recognition of the Brotherhood of Man." The members of this society subscribe to the following pledge: "I, the undersigned, promise to help in securing to every member of the human family freedom, equal opportunity, and brotherly consideration." Hundreds of names were enrolled at each meeting, and the strongest resolutions of condemnation and protest were passed after hearing my narration of the lynchings in the States. They felt it to be their duty to express in the strongest terms denunciation of the burning alive of human beings and the lawless wholesale hanging of the same. The leading newspapers of the United Kingdom gave excellent reports of the meetings, and many of them ringing and outspoken editorials against this state of affairs. The two months' tour closed, and I returned to the United States.

In Pembroke Chapel.

The Society for the Recognition of the Brotherhood of Man, feeling that my first visit was not as thorough in its results as could be wished, invited me again this year to prosecute the work. I landed from the Germanic Friday last, and immediately received an invitation to address the congregation of Pembroke Chapel Sunday evening. The pastor, Rev. C. G. Aked, who is mine host, is one of the most advanced thinkers in the pulpit of today and has the largest nonconformist congregation outside of London. He had already chosen for his Sunday evening discourse the subject "An Enemy of the People," and the discussion was devoted to Ibsen's drama of that name and the lessons to be deduced therefrom.

14

After service he dismissed those who wished to go, and invited the others to hear my story. Nearly every one of those 1,200 remained. Rev. Aked then said that when I was in Liverpool last year friends of his who had heard me speak in London and other places in Liverpool wished him to invite me to speak in his church. He refused because he didn't know me nor believe what I said was true. Since that time he had been to America and was in Chicago to see the World's Fair, the first week in July. He there read confirmation of all I had said in the reports of the Miller lynching case in Bardwell, Ky., July 7. "First," he said, "came the report that the Ray girls had been murdered and a negro was suspected; next that they had bloodhounds on his track; then they had caught the murderer and were going to roast him alive at 3 o'clock that afternoon, although he protested his innocence in an earnest, straightforward account of his movements. I sat under the shadow of the statue of Liberty in Jackson Park and read these accounts until I was wild. I saw that 40,000,000 people read the same horrible story of the mob's hunt and openly expressed intention three days before the lynching, and nobody lifted a hand to prevent it. When I read next morning that the mob became impatient and hurried the prisoner out and lynched him before 3 o'clock that memorable July 7 I knew that what Miss Wells said was true, and before I had left the United States already there had been enough evidence to show that they had lynched the wrong man."

A Splendid Opportunity.

To this confirmation of my story then I owed the

hearty reception and most splendid opportunity to appeal to English people to aid us in molding American public sentiment in favor of justice to every one, and a fair trial for life and liberty. Mr. Aked was the guest of Mrs. Henry Ward Beecher while in Brooklyn last summer and preached three of the four Sundays he was in the United States at Beecher's church. It was here in Liverpool, by the way, where Henry Ward Beecher was mobbed when he tried to speak on anti-slavery subjects in the '40s. The sentiment in Liverpool was strongly pro-slavery, for was not Liverpool the greatest cotton market in the world, and if slavery was abolished would not that interfere with the cotton market? It was with this part of England as with the weak-kneed North preceding the war – a disturbance of the institution meant a possible depletion of their purses, and so they were in favor of its continuance. It is related of a London actor who came on the stage drunk while in Liverpool that the audience hissed him. He straightened up as well as an intoxicated man could and in his deepest voice cried out, "What! Have I come from London to be hissed by you; *you*, every brick in whose walls is cemented by the blood of slaves?" and the hissing ceased long before the scornful tones had stopped reverberating.

Sir Edward Russell.

But Liverpool has long since redeemed herself, and no larger or more sympathetic audiences will greet me anywhere than in this same city. Sir Edward Russell, the editor of the Liverpool *Post* and one of the ablest in the kingdom, accorded me an interview last year, and since then has devoted much space in his paper to

16

the subject of lynch law. He sent a cordial note of approval to Mr. Aked for his invitation to me, and added: "There is no subject upon which the civilized world needs more to be aroused than that of lynching." A large meeting in one of the town halls is being arranged for, and Sir Edward Russell is to preside.

The question has been asked by Americans why I come abroad to tell of the race's grievances, and if more good might not be done in America? Unquestionably, if the same opportunity were afforded us to be heard, but we, as a race, cannot get a hearing in the United States. The statistics show that lynchings for 1893 were as frequent and some of them more shocking than the year previous. The press and pulpit of the country are practically silent with a silence which means encouragement. The pages of current literature, when opened to a discussion of the negro question at all, are open only to the Southern white man, who is given full license to defame the entire negro race as he chooses. Bishop Haygood, Bill Arp, and others of their ilk have been given full swing in that direction and no opportunity accorded the race villified to defend itself. These agencies seem to have redoubled their efforts to murder the negro and blast his reputation, and we feel driven to do the same in our own defence, and the society for the recognition of the brotherhood of man in England and Scotland forms the only opening. As the English press and pulpit set the example in speaking out plainly against such injustice, it is to be hoped that these powerful agencies in the United States will do the same. When they do sentiment will be aroused and laws enacted which will put a stop to America's disgrace.   IDA B. WELLS.

IDA B. WELLS ABROAD.

Speaking in Liverpool Against Lynchers of Negroes.

BRITISH SENTIMENT.

How the Chicago of England Learned a Lesson.

A Photograph Sent Out by Lynchers Brought Up
in Evidence Against Them.

LIVERPOOL, March 24.* – *Special Correspondence.* – Liverpool was the center of slave interests from the days of good Queen Bess to the abolition of slavery by the British in 1807. More than half the slave ships which carried human merchandise from Africa to the West Indies and America were built in the Liverpool docks and owned by Liverpool merchants. The triple voyages of these ships brought enormous wealth to the owners and to the city. There was first the voyage to Africa, where hundreds of slaves were captured or bought for a few gewgaws; thence to the West Indies, where the cargo was sold at 100 per cent profit, and the ship's hold stored with sugar and rum; this at Liverpool brought as great profit as had the slaves in the West Indies. The opposition to the abolition of the slave trade as a matter of course came from those who profited most largely by it. Right finally prevailed, and Liverpool in 1806 returned as its member of Parliament a man who had written the first philippic against slavery thirty years before. William Roscoe aided materially in the passage of the bill for the abolition of slavery.

In 1861, fifty-five years later, the strongest sympathy evinced for the pro-slavery party in the United States was found in Liverpool. After the cessation of its own slave trade the shipping merchants and cotton mills had gradually built up a flourishing trade in the cotton produced by slave labor in the Southern States.

The Southern ports were blockaded and no more cotton could be obtained. The ships were idle and the looms empty. Again self-interest pointed the way, and Liverpudlians gave their support to the South. Hon. W. E. Gladstone, a native of Liverpool, whose wealth had come from slave labor on a West India plantation, and who was then leader of the House of Commons, said concerning secession: "Jeff Davis has created a nation." In the Liverpool docks were built the gunboats Florida and Alabama, which saw such active service in the Confederate cause. Here it was that Henry Ward Beecher met the greatest resistance to his attempts to speak in behalf of the Union in 1863. For nearly three hours the mob at the Philharmonic Hall yelled, hisses, hooted, and interrupted him when he began to speak, but he managed little by little to get his address all out at last.

What Liverpool Has Learned.

But Liverpool has learned that she can prosper

without the slave trade or slave labor. Her docks are crowded with shipping from all parts of the world, and the city, with its population of 600,000 souls, is one of the most prosperous in the United Kingdom. Her freedom-loving citizens not only subscribe to the doctrine that human beings regardless of color or condition, are equal before the law, but they practice as they preach. To a colored person who has been reared in the peculiar atmosphere which obtains only in free (?) America, it is like being born into another world, to be welcomed among persons of the highest order of intellectual and social culture as if one were one of themselves. Here a "colored" person can ride in any sort of conveyance in any part of the country without being insulted, stop at any hotel, or be accommodated at any restaurant one wishes without being refused with contempt; wander into any picture gallery, lecture-room, concert hall, theater, or church and receive only the most courteous treatment from officials and fellow sightseers. The privilege of being once in a country where "man's a man for a' that" is one which can best be appreciated by those Americans whose black skins are a bar to them receiving genuine courtesy and kindliness at home.

I have spent two weeks in Liverpool and have delivered by invitation ten addresses on "Lynch Law in the United States." These meetings have averaged 1,000 persons each, and though I grieved to have to do so, yet truth compelled me to say that lynch law is spreading in the States. Illinois, Indiana, Ohio, Iowa, and Pennsylvania have each had lynchings within the past nine months, and nothing more has been done to punish lynchers in these States than in the States south of Mason and Dixon's line. I take the statistics of lynchings and prove that according to the charges given not one-third of the men and women lynched are charged with assault on white women, and brand that statement as a falsehood invented by the lynchers to justify acts of cruelty and outrage. I find wherever I go that we are deprived the expression of condemnation such hangings and burnings deserve, because the world believes negro men are despoilers of the virtue of white women.

A Picture.

Unfortunately for the negro race and for themselves, Miss Frances E. Willard and Bishops Fitzgerald and Haygood have published utterances in confirmation of this slander, and the magazines of my country have printed his libel on an entire race to the four corners of the earth. Whatever is lacking in these articles is supplied by the white American individual abroad. He draws a picture of the isolated districts in the South where great hordes of ignorant and dangerous negroes swarm, of the inadequacy and delay of the law, and then asks: "What would you do if your wife or daughter were so assaulted?" And the person for whose benefit this picture is drawn finds himself relenting in his judgment and he remains silent when he meant to condemn burning and hanging.

Finding that such a picture is drawn, I am thus forced to draw another and show (1) that all the machinery of law and politics is in the hands of those who commit the lynchings; they, therefore, have the amending of the laws in their own hands; and that it is only wealthy white men whom the law fails to reach, in every case of criminal procedure the negro is punished. 2. Hundreds of negroes, including women and children, are lynched for trivial offenses, on suspicion, and in many cases when known to be guiltless of any crime and the law refuses to punish the murderers because it is not considered a crime to kill a negro. 3. Many of the cases of "assault" are simple adultery between white women and colored men. The Society for the Furtherance of Human Brotherhood hopes first to arouse public sentiment by making known the facts of the lynching infamy, then to appeal to American honor through the various Christian philanthropic and temperance organizations of this country to remove the stain against its Christianity and civilization by putting down mob law and establishing it as a fact as well as a theory that every man shall be tried by law and punished by the same agency for any crime he commits.

The Sympathetic Audiences.

I spoke in Pembroke Chapel the first Sunday night of my stay in Liverpool, and the pastor of the church, Rev. C. F. Aked, presided. Last Sunday afternoon to an audience of 1,500 men in the Congregational Church. Sunday night at the Unitarian Church, after service, Rev. R. A. Armstrong presiding. The Lord Mayor of Liverpool is a member of this congregation, and consented at first to preside but was prevented from so doing. At a monster meeting in honor of the ninetieth birthday of General Neal Dow Tuesday, March 20 I spoke again, and the storms of applause convinced me of the sympathy of the audience. Every newspaper in the city has contained full accounts of the meetings and several strong editorials have been written. When our own newspapers in season and out do so, lynch law will soon become infamous.

Not only have the daily and weekly newspapers given such space to the subject, but the editor of the *Daily Post*, Sir Edward Russell, presided over the large meeting held at Hope Hall Thursday night, March 22. This gentleman is the most prominent and influential citizen in Liverpool today, and his time is fully occupied with his literary, social, and political pursuits. Yet he has taken deep interest in this question ever since he saw a cut of the photograph of a lynching sent Judge Tourgee nearly three years ago by the Christians of Clanton, Ala. It will be remembered that a negro was lynched in that town, August, 1891; that the mob ranged itself under the body of the man as he hung and was photographed; and that photograph was sent to Judge Tourgee, with the following message on the back: "This ---- ---- was hung at Clanton, Ala., Friday, Aug. 21, 1891, for murdering a little white boy in cold blood for 35 cents in cash. He is a good specimen of your black Christians hung by white heathens. With compliments of the committee."

Lyncher Against Lyncher.

This photograph represented boys from 10 years old upward standing under the ghastly object. An English lady, who published a little journal called *Anti-Caste*, had a cut made from this photograph and reproduced it in her paper. When Sir Edward Russell saw a copy of it he wrote an editorial protesting against it as an illustration drawn from the imagination, and was horrified to be told that it was a photograph taken from life and

sent out by the lynchers themselves. From that moment dates his interest in the subject. He thinks it the
one subject upon which the sympathies of the world
need arousing.

The following account is taken from the *Daily Post*
of next morning, and it is submitted because the full
text of Sir Edward Russell's address is given, together
with the resolution which was passed by the meeting.
This resolution is the same in tenor as those passed at
other meetings:

Last evening, in Hope Hall, Hope street, Miss Ida
Wells, colored editress of *Free Speech*, lectured to a large
and enthusiastic auditory on the subject of "American
Atrocities."

Sir Edward Russell presided, and in introducing
the lecturer, after devotional exercises, said it was the
function of those who, like himself, were not specially
informed upon the subject to hear rather than to speak.
They were present to listen to the testimony of a distinguished lady. [Applause.] It was important to know
whom they were to hear, and why; and when they
heard Miss Wells he hoped they would say that she
was adorned by every grace of womanhood, and justified by her abilities the public duty which she had un-
dertaken, having been provoked into appealing to the
public opinion of this country by acts which they must
all deplore, and of which they should be glad to make
some people ashamed. [Applause.] At the outset they
were confronted with the objection that it was scarcely
a fit thing for the people of one country to pronounce
upon the misdeeds of the people of another. He was
afraid, however, that it was rather late in the day for
English people to stop short at such an objection as

that. [Hear, hear.] We had our own faults, but it had never been one of these to hold our tongues about the iniquities of other people. [Laughter.]

England's Sacrifice.

We had an honorable pre-eminence in this matter of the war of the races, because this country made an un-exampled sacrifice by a heroic declaration, expression, and enactment of its will which had entitled Great Brit-ain to speak on the subject of the colored races wher-ever their liberties were interfered with. They were glad to believe, also, that they had many friends in America, and that there were many consciences in that country which were not unwilling to listen to the testi-mony of the English race when directed against things which had an iniquitous aspect in reference to the col-ored race. For many, many years the sympathy of the English nation for those who wished to emancipate the colored race was the one great strength of the aboli-tionists of America [hear, hear], and now that the old days of slavery had passed away, but had left behind them liabilities to injustice and even to bloodshed, they might fairly step into the arena again, so as to see if they could not yet accomplish something for the good old cause. They had in this matter two things to con-sider. The first was the existence of lynch law in a civi-lized country, and the second the especial application of it to the colored people of America. Either of these things was a very fair subject for protest. For his own part, he would say without qualification that he could not imagine a crime so great that it need be avenged by lynch law in any country in the world (hear, hear); and, what was more, he did not believe that crime ever was avenged by lynch law without a lowering of the moral tone of the community, and without the introduction of worse evils than were attempted to be suppressed. [Applause.]

The Worst Phase.

The worst of it was, too, that lynch law was directed against persons very largely defenseless, and more or less under a social ban, afflicted by disabilities, and always under a very fatal disadvantage of race prejudice. It would therefore, be a very great thing if everybody in that hall, and those who came to know of their proceedings, were to form a resolution that from now to the day of their death any injustice founded upon prejudice against race should be dismissed from the mind as being beneath contempt (hear, hear); as consistent with the Christian character, and even incompatible with civilization [Applause.]

Miss Wells, who was very cordially received, narrated in her own quiet and unimpassioned but earnest and forcible way her tale of lynching atrocities perpetrated in recent years against the people of her race in America and the operation of the social prejudices directed against them. In the course of her address she paid to Chicago the tribute of being the freest city in America in expression of opinion in favor of the negro. [Applause.]

Rev. C. F. Aked moved: "This meeting having heard from Miss Ida B. Wells, with the deepest pain, a recital of the wrongs done to the colored people of the Southern States of America by lawless mobs, and having in mind the confirmation of Miss Wells' story supplied with lamentable frequency by the press of the United

States and Great Britain, expresses the opinion that the perpetration of such outrages unchecked by the civil power must necessarily reflect upon the administration of justice in the United States and upon the honor of its people." [Applause.] In advocating the cause Mr. Aked said that lynching, however bad for the negro, was still worse for those who did it.

The Results of War.

Mr. S. J. Celestine Edwards, a colored man, in seconding the proposition, maintained that war had never ended anything so as to permanently satisfy both the conquered and the conquerer. [Hear, Hear.] The Southerners of America had never been satisfied with the defeat they had sustained at the hands of the Northerners and the loss of their property in negroes. This had been a thorn in their flesh for years, and he held that they would never succeed in ameliorating the conditions under which his race labored until the remnant of the old Abolitionists of America began the work where they had left it off when the civil war began. The Northerners, he acknowledged, had always been tolerant of negro competition, but the Southern whites could never abide it. As an instance of the prejudice existing against his people, he said that when a well-to-do negro took his invalid wife to Louisiana the white citizens demanded his expulsion, his only crime being that he was the richest man among them. They had white friends working in their cause in America, and British sympathy would greatly strengthen them and hasten the time when the negroes would be properly emancipated. He argued that whatever might be said about the laziness of the negro, he was not nearly so vicious as the European.

Rev. W. W. Howard, in supporting, spoke of the Liverpool *Daily Post* as having first taken up the questions of temperance and social purity, and now it was taking up another great question.

The resolution was carried with great enthusiasm.

The Liverpool *Mercury,* which is the other leading daily of the city, contained a strong leader of more than a column on the subject. From Liverpool I go to Manchester, where large meetings have been arranged.

IDA B. WELLS.

IDA B. WELLS ABROAD.

The Bishop of Manchester on American Lynching.

ITS HORRIBLE CRUELTIES.

England Sympathizes with the African Race.

Description of Attitude of Moody and Miss Willard
to the Negroes. - Description of England's "Big Ditch."

MANCHESTER, England, April 4.* – *Special Correspondence.* – Until the first of this year Manchester has been an inland town, thirty-five miles from the sea. By means of the ship canal she is now in direct communication with the sea, and therefore independent of Liverpool, her great rival in point of size, wealth, etc. Liverpool has few manufacturing interests – her importance is derived from her situation as a seaport; her life is purely commercial, and her wealth derived from handling the produce of other towns and countries, so the citizen of Manchester will tell you. Manchester, on the other hand, is an enormous manufacturing center. There are near 500 cotton spinning firms in and around the city and these own over 18,000,000 spindles, more than one-third of all those in Great Britain. There are chemical works and great engineering factories, and the export and import trade of these industries is of great magnitude. Liverpool and the railways made their burdens too grievous to be borne, besides diverting this trade from Manchester, and the ship canal is the result.

The largest ships bringing produce, cotton, and iron to the markets and mills need not now wait in vexatious delay outside Liverpool to be docked, but steaming up the canal, reach Manchester as quickly as they can be unloaded from the vessels and onto the railways at Liverpool. In return manufacturers can ship machinery and cotton goods to all parts of the world, direct from Manchester factories, and at far less cost and delay. Manchester is jubilant over its emancipation, and Liverpool consoles itself for the loss of this great trade by speaking contemptuously of the "Big Ditch."

The Great Canal.

It is more than a big ditch, as will be seen by the most skeptical person who takes a ride along its thirty-five miles of waterway and observes what engineering skill and patient plodding have accomplished. Where there was formerly a small stream of water winding in and out toward the sea there is now a broad, deep channel, twice the width of the Suez Canal, and any two of the largest vessels afloat can sail together abreast along its waters.

This canal, which has been open to traffic only three months, is the realization of an idea nearly 180 years old, for it was first suggested in 1710. The plan came up for consideration from time to time, until in 1877 it assumed concrete shape, and in 1882 a bill was laid before Parliament by a committee of merchants and manufacturers for permission to construct the canal. The bill was bitterly opposed by the dock and railway companies of Liverpool. It took three years to overcome opposition and secure the grant from Parliament; it required another three years to secure sufficient capital to undertake the work and the remaining five years in which to actually do the work and realize the dreams of the promoters. Not only is the canal dotted with ships bearing freight from all parts of the world, but passenger steamers also. The America and Australia go up and down its length, and when the smell is less suggestive of the Chicago River the ride on this artificial waterway will be much more pleasant than it is at present.

The Queen to Open the Canal.

Her gracious Majesty, Queen Victoria, appreciating the success of this, one of the most gigantic of modern undertakings, will come to Manchester in June to formally open the canal. Manchester people are making huge preparations to celebrate the completion of what has cost them $75,000,000, and the celebration promises to be the success so magnificent an undertaking deserves.

The city proper of Manchester claims nearly 600,000 inhabitants. Her immediate suburban towns, especially Salford, give her a population of a million and a half souls. Though each one maintains its own city government, one cannot easily tell where Manchester ends and Salford, Rusholme, Ancoats and Ashton begin. The main streets are named after London, for Piccadilly and Pall Mall are as familiar to Manchester localities as London. Her public buildings, like those of most English towns, have stood for years and are black with the century's smoke and dust; and very few know the use of paint. Her art galleries are so arranged that the frame of every picture is plainly seen, and one has no need of a catalogue to pick out name and artist. This is a convenience to the general public which other art galleries, which shall be nameless, might copy to advantage. To her treasures of art Manchester has lately added Mr. Watts' latest picture, "The Good Samaritan."

American Lynching Condemned.

The feeling which developed in Liverpool during the American civil war was shared in large measure and for the same reasons (the injury to the cotton trade) by the people of Manchester. In this city also Rev. Henry Ward Beecher fought one of his hard-won battles on the lecture platform with the mob of pro-slavery and secession sympathizers. But that is all past. The freedom of her public halls, church platforms, and the press is cheerfully granted to those who speak for justice and fair play to the oppressed.

From the Bishop of Manchester, the Society of Friends, Unitarians, Methodists, and Congregationalists, American lynching has received not only strong words of condemnation, but earnest resolutions have been passed in a spirit of Christian love, calling upon the people of the United States to remove the blot upon their good name and put a stop to our "national crime."

A Letter to the Christian Register.

The following letter addressed to the *Christian Reg-*

ister, the leading Unitarian organ of the United States, was published in a daily paper here this week:

Dear Sir – Last Sunday evening, after our usual service, Miss Ida B. Wells told my congregation the story of the lynchings in your Southern States. My church is the historic Church of James Martineau and William Henry Channing, and we believe that we were on the line of our best traditions in giving the platform to a lady who told us that she wished to plead for justice and for mercy. She spoke with singular refinement, dignity, and self-restraint, nor have I ever met any other "agitator" so cautious and unimpassioned in speech. But by this marvelous self-restraint itself she moved us all the more profoundly. When she sat down we resolved with solemn unanimity – "That we, who are this evening assembled in Hope Street Church, learn with grief and horror of the barbarities of lynch law as carried out by white men on some of the colored citizens of the United States, and that, in the name of our common humanity we call on all lovers of justice, of freedom, and of brotherhood among our kinsmen in the States to determine that these things shall no more be." We know, dear New England brothers and sisters, that remonstrance addressed by members of one nationality to the people of another can only be justified in the rarest cases and that there is always danger that such remonstrance will rather stir up resentment than achieve its purpose. Yet in the face of the terrible facts we cannot do other than plead with you to bestir yourselves to save the good name of your nation. When I think of the strong men and the gracious ladies I met in Boston, and their generous culture, of their wide and noble views on social problems, of their high and pure Christianity, of their devoted lives, I am bewildered to be told that people such as these will not listen to the pleadings of those who are denied the ordinary securities of law, that they are passive in the view of sickening brutalities, that they are silent when their fellow citizens are scourged and flayed and burnt without trial or appeal. I know well what you of the North have suffered for the slave. Was it for this that with so supreme a courage you carried through your colossal war? I know, too, the jealousy with which State rights are guarded and your wise reluctance to interfere with the domestic usages of sister States. Yet can I not believe that free murder is among those State rights with which the national legislature cannot concern itself or the national conscience be aroused. What are you doing, men and women of Boston? Are you so busy laying wreaths on the tombs of Channing and of Parker, of brave John Brown and your immortal Garrison, that you have no time to head the seizure of untried men and women, their execution with every devise and torture, and acquiescence of all the guardians of the law, the instilling into the boys and girls of the United States of the lust of cruelty and callousness to murder? What meant the marvelous parliament of religions at Chicago with its astounding manifestation of a world-wide human brotherhood if the negro on your own soil – nay, the mulatto in whose veins flows as much Anglo-Saxon blood as African – can find beneath your national flag no security against the brutality of lawless mobs and the nameless horrors of the amateur scaffold, the branding iron and the stake? In great disturbance of soul I am, dear sir, faithfully yours.

RICHARD ACLAND ARMSTRONG.

Liverpool, March 21.

Twelve Lectures in Ten Days.

The same matter will be brought before the national conference of Unitarians, which meets in Manchester next week. I have spoken twelve times during my ten days' stay in Manchester. Three of these were drawing-room meetings in the homes of as many of Manchester's wealthy citizens; one was in the town hall, three in churches, and five in public halls. There were accounts of recent lynchings in the afternoon papers, which were read at two of my meetings as emphasis to what I had told them. I had seen the account of the colored woman who was found hanging to a tree in Little Rock, Ark., about which nobody, as usual, seemed to know anything; but I did not know of the horrible case of the woman in San Antonio, Texas, who had been boxed up in a barrel with nails driven through the sides and rolled down hill till she was dead.

A gentleman who was principal of the city school rose and read the account after my address. He had brought the afternoon paper to read on his way to the meeting, and this lynching was the first thing he saw as he opened the paper. And I sat there as if turned to stone, with the tears rolling down my cheeks at this new evidence of outrage upon my people and apathy of the American white people.

Mr. Axon Speaks of Slavery.

My first big meeting in this city was presided over by Mr. W. E. A. Axon, one of the editors of the Manchester *Guardian*, a visitor to the World's Fair, and delegate to the vegetarian congress last year. He is my host, and had found sad confirmation of all I said when here last year, when he was in the States. At the next important

37

meeting the chair was taken by Rev. S. A. Steinthal, well known in Boston as the friend of Garrison and a member of the Anti-Slavery Society. He was a delegate to the Parliament of Religions at Chicago, and in his address, on introducing me, he told how surprised he was to find people in the North excusing and condoning lynching; that he was at a railway station called Winetka, a few miles out from Chicago, when a fresh lynching was being discussed, and he was astounded to find every white man present approved of it! So much so that, stranger as he was, he was compelled to express himself to those advocates of lawlessness, and say to them that nothing justified such lawlessness.

A Leader in the Guardian.

The Manchester *Guardian* of March 30 contained the following significant leader on the encroachments of the mob on Northern territory:

Lynch law has long been an unenviable, characteristic of the Southern States of America, but it appears to be infecting the North also. There were lynchings in Illinois whilst the Chicago Exposition was inviting the attention of the world to the products of American civilization. In the present month not only Tennessee but Pennsylvania has shown the ghastly spectacle of human beings put to an ignominious death without any form of trial. The victims of these outrages are usually persons of negro blood. As the whole machinery of law and justice is in the hands of the whites there can be no pretense that there would be any likelihood of the escape of those whose guilt could be reasonably established. These ghastly murders are in fact, the outcome of the race prejudice which has survived from the days of slavery. The average American protests that all men are "born free and equal," but denies in practice the commonest rights of humanity to all American citizens who have any negro blood in their veins. How the matter appears to the intelligent and educated Afro-Americans may be seen from the public utterances of Miss Ida B. Wells, who is now on a second visit to England. Her indictment is all the more telling from the absence of rhetoric. The negro race has made great progress since the war in intelligence, refinement, and wealth, but everywhere the brazen wall of prejudice shuts him out from the common inheritance. The "color line" is sharply drawn in the churches, the professions, the trades, and industries of America. In the South he may not enter the white man's church, school, college, or even railway carriage. There is perhaps a contemptuous kindliness for him so long as he remains a hewer of wood and drawer of water, with no aspirations or with aspirations carefully suppressed, but so soon as he claims the position of a citizen of a free country the whole force of social pressure is exerted to keep him down. The hangings, shootings, burnings of negros who have not been convicted of any crime bring discredit upon the American Nation, and those who take part in these murders or condone them are the deadliest foes of those free institutions of which America claims to be in a special sense the home.

The Voice of the "Bystander."
Will the American Nation heed these utterances made by those who love her, and are proud of her achievements? It is earnestly to be hoped so, since I can point to nothing which has been done heretofore

on this score save the voice of the "Bystander," which has been heard so long through the columns of THE INTER OCEAN. He only has insisted on justice full and free to every American citizen.

I have been asked as to the attitude of Rev. Dwight L. Moody and Miss Frances E. Willard, both well known in Great Britain, on this subject of the negro's rights. I have been compelled in the interest of truth to say that they have given the weight of their influence to the Southern white man's prejudices. Mr. Moody has encouraged the drawing of the color line in the churches by consenting to preach on a separate day and in a separate church to the colored people in his tours through the South.

Miss Willard's Attitude to the Colored Race.

Miss Willard has gone even further in that she has put herself on record as approving the Southerner's method of defying the constitution and suppressing the negro vote; has promised that "when I go North there will be no word wafted to you from pen or voice that is not loyal to what we are saying here and now"; has unhesitatingly sown broadcast a slander against the entire negro race in order to gain favor with those who are hanging, shooting, and burning negroes alive. This she did in an interview published in the *Voice*, New York city. Oct. 23, 1890. In it she speaks of "great dark-faced mobs, whose rallying cry is better whisky and more of it. * * * The grogshop is their center of power. The safety of woman, of childhood, of the home is menaced in a thousand localities at this moment, so that men dare not go beyond the sight of their own rooftree."

The South Encouraged in Cruelty.

Because of such utterances the South is encouraged and justified in its work of disgracing the Nation, and the world is confirmed in the belief that the negro race is the most degraded on the face of the earth. Those who read and accept this last-quoted statement forget that these same white men were not afraid to go beyond the sight of their rooftrees during the civil war and leave the safety and honor of their homes, their wives, daughters, and sisters only in the protection of the negro race.

But I do not need here to declare the statement a false one. Hon. Frederick Douglass has already done that. I am only to tell here what truth has compelled me to say as to the words and actions of some of our American Christian and temperance workers when asked by English friends to do so.

IDA B. WELLS.

IDA B. WELLS ABROAD.

Lectures in Bristol, England, on American Lynch Law.

AUDIENCES ARE SHOCKED.

Very Pleasant Afternoon with Lady Jeune.

Cordial Receptions from Churches of All
Denominations – Horrified at Cruelties Perpetrated.

NEWCASTLE, April 23* – *Special Correspondence.* – Since my last letter from Manchester I have been so constantly traveling and speaking that I could not write. From Manchester I went to Southport and spoke to an audience of near 2,000 persons. Rev. J. J. Fitch presided and the three newspapers gave an extended report and the audience passed a strong resolution of condemnation of lynching in some strong speeches that were made. The resolution was seconded by Mrs. Callender Moss, a charming speaker and a prominent member of the British Women's Liberal Association. I was the guest of an able English authoress, "Evan May." I could only stay the one night, so am to return in June and speak for the Women's Liberal Association and another meeting arranged by the Misses Ryley, the wealthiest women in the town, and whose guest I am to be. From Southport I went to Bristol, that old historic town, and spent a week, speaking on an average of twice a day.

Horrified at the Negro Lynchings.

There were two drawing-room meetings at the homes of wealthy and influential persons. In these drawing-rooms, in which there were 100 persons each, were gathered the wealthiest and most cultured classes of society who do not attend public meetings. One was presided over by Dr. Miller Nicholson, the pastor of the largest and most influential Presbyterian Church in the city, and the other by Mrs. Coote, president of the Women's Liberal Association of Bristol. Their shock on being told the actual condition of things regarding lynching was painful to behold. Most of them, as they said in their speeches, had imagined that since emancipation the negroes were in the enjoyment of all their rights. It is true they had read of lynchings, and while they thought them dreadful had accepted the general belief that it was for terrible crimes perpetrated by negro men upon white women. I read the account of that poor woman who was boxed up in the barrel into which nails had been driven and rolled down hill in Texas, and asked if that lynching could be excused on the same ground.

The Troublesome Question Ignored.

Again the question was asked where was all the legal and civil authority of the country, to say nothing of the Christian churches, that they permitted such things to be. And I could only say that, despite the axiom that there is a remedy for every wrong, everybody in authority, from the President of the United States down, had declared their inability to do anything, and that the Christian bodies and moral associations would not touch the question. It's the easiest way to get along with the South (and those portions of the North where lynchings take place) to ignore the question altogether, and it is done; they are too busy saving the souls of white Christians from future burning in hell-fire to save the lives of black ones from present burning in flames kindled by the white Christians. The feelings of the people who do these acts must not be hurt by protesting against this sort of thing, and so the bodies of the victims of mob hate must be sacrificed, and the country disgraced, because of that fear to speak out.

Negro Communicants Refused Seats.

It seems especially incredible to them that the Christian churches of the South refuse to admit negro communicants into their houses of worship save in the galleries or on the back seats. When I was told of a young mulatto man named James Cotton, who was dragged out of one of the leading churches in Memphis, Tenn., by a policeman and shut up in the stationhouse all day Sunday for taking a seat in the church, one lady remarked that it was easy to believe anything after that. I was asked if the Northern churches knew of this discrimination and continued fellowship with the churches which practiced it. Truth compelled me to reply in the affirmative, and to give instances which showed that in every case the Northern churches, which do not practice these things themselves, tacitly agreed to them by the Southern churches; and that so far as I knew principle has always yielded to prejudice in the hope of gaining the good will of the South. I had especially in mind the national Baptist convention which met in Philadelphia June 1892. An effort was made to have a resolution passed by the convention condemning lynching, as the Methodist Episcopal general conference had done at Omaha in May. The committee on resolutions decided that it could not be done, as they had too many Southern delegates present and they did not wish to offend them.

The Y. M. C. A. Has No Colored Delegates.

A clergyman of the Church of England who was present while [he] was in America a few years ago visiting at Mr. Moody's home, Northfield, Mass., he attended a national convention of the Y. M.C.A. and after it was over, being disappointed in seeing no colored delegates, asked if there were none who were members. He was told that there had been a few in previous meetings, but this particular year (I forget which one) special efforts had been made to get Southern delegates to be present, so no colored ones had been invited. These were the only terms upon which the Y.M.C.A. and the W. C. T. U. had obtained a foothold in the South, and they had consented to the arrangement which shut the negro out. They continually declared the negro degraded, intemperate, and wicked, and yet shut him out from all influences in which he might become better. The American press was little better. Now and then, when a particularly horrible case of lynching was reported, there were strong editorials against it, and then the subject died away. The New York *Independent* and the *Forum* had symposiums lately on the subject in which the Southern white man had vented his opinion fully and freely, and the *Independent* had been good enough to give the negro a voice in the discussion.

The Inter Ocean Gives Fair Play.

Only THE INTER OCEAN among the dailies and Judge A. W. Tourgee as an individual had given any systematic attention and discussion to the subject from the standpoint of equal and exact justice to all in the condemnation of lynching. On behalf of my race I am glad of every opportunity to bear testimony to the work of these two powerful advocates, and especially the former for giving the negro a chance to be heard in his own behalf.

I spoke ten times in Bristol during my week's stay – at two Congregational, two Baptist, and two Wesleyan churches, and a large public meeting in the Y.M.C.A. Hall. This meeting was presided over by Rev. G. Arthur Sowter, rector of the largest parish in Bristol, a Church of England clergyman. Young, ardent, and enthusiastic, he made a most glowing speech after leading me on the platform. I spoke an hour and a half, and not a person in that vast audience moved.

White-Cap Outrages.

I forgot time and place for again news had reached me of the work of the mob known as white caps on the negro, Alex Johnson, and of the lynching of the little 13-year-old negro boy who was charged with killing the sheriff. How long, oh, how long shall we have to suffer these things? The country owes something to the negro for his very forbearance. He has never given trouble, as the strikers and anarchists. The American dispatches in the English press tell how members of Congress, prominent citizens, women, and legal authorities are exercising themselves on behalf of the "Coxeyites" and other agitators. Nobody is moving a finger to stay these outrages upon negroes. No wonder the Liverpool *Daily Post* of April 19 devotes a column-and-a-half editorial to surprise at this apathy, and condemnation of the lynchings which take place with such regularity.

Great Nations Shame Each Other.

Sir Edward Russell in that editorial said: "Certain fears seem to be entertained that if we as a nation rebuked the Americans too plainly for their tolerance of lynch law they might turn upon us with the retaliation that we still permit the sweating system to hold its sway. Let them. It is an essential part of the business of great nations to shame each other, and if sweating is a preventable evil – which does not quite appear – let the Americans shame us into preventing it. They are in the meanwhile horrifying the whole of the civilized world by allowing law to be ignored, justice to be disgraced, and humanity outraged by continuous exhibitions of reckless popular brutality, which, to all appearance, in five cases out of ten do not even correspond with the rough justice of the case." Quoting Mr. Aked's article in the *Christian World* of last week, anent the C. J. Miller case, the *Post* continues: "Such things as these curdle the blood when read about in the books of adventure and sensation that have been written about the lawless West; but when one reflects that they still happen while we in this country are sending missions to the South

Sea Islands and other places, they strike to our hearts much more forcibly, and we turn over in our minds whether it were not better to leave the heathen alone for a time and to send the gospel of common humanity across the Atlantic, which is now a five days' journey."

A Movement Condemning Lynching.

An effort is being made, seconded by the great Dr. Clifford, to pass a resolution before the National Baptist Union, which meets in London this week, condemning lynching. The *Christian World*, the leading religious journal of the kingdom, gives notice of the resolution and says editorially: "It is earnestly to be hoped that the voice of England will help the better feeling of America so to assert itself as to bring to a speedy end a state of things which, if the published reports be correct, would disgrace a nation of cannibals." The resolution at the Bristol meeting was seconded by the great Dr. Culross, president of the Baptist College at that place, and a pulpit representative of every denomination in the city sat on the platform at that meeting. I spoke also before the Bristol Congregational Ministers' Union and the quarterly meeting of the Quakers from the two counties. That was a large gathering of 500, and as the men and women meet in separate rooms to transact their business, I was given an opportunity to speak after dinner in the long dining hall before they left the tables. They then decided to have a joint meeting, and in that meeting recommended me to the yearly meeting at London, and asked that mention be made in the yearly epistles to American Quakers urging them to take some steps to put down lynching, especially as one of the last lynchings was reported from

Pennsylvania, the Quaker State.

From Bristol I went to Newbury, a small town of 11,000 inhabitants in Gloucestershire, by invitation to hold two meetings. Here the meeting was presided over by the mayor of the town, Mr. Elliott, who feels most strongly on the lynching question. The meeting was characterized by the exhibition of strong feeling.

Afternoon Tea at Lady Jeune's.

Here through the good influences of the mayor, who drove me out to her ladyship's country seat, I met Lady Jeune, wife of Sir Francis Jeune, one of the most eminent jurists on the bench in the United Kingdom, and Mr. Elliott tells me that her ladyship is one of the most influential and cultured women of the British aristocracy. It was Saturday evening and Lord Randolph Churchill and other nobles had just gone – having been Lady Jeune's guests for the week. She had given orders that she was not at home, but when the footman took in Mr. Elliott's card she came to the door to welcome us, invited us to tea with herself and children, and had me tell her all about it. She, too, was glad to be enlightened on the lynching mania, and shocked for the sake of humanity. When I go up to London next week she will have a drawing-room meeting of her friends, for she thinks they ought to know that the negro race is not the degraded one she has been led to believe.

From Newbury to Newcastle, in the north of England, is a long journey, as English journeys go, of ten hours. But there are important engagements which must be filled before I go to London. Here again I meet the terrible impression that the negro race is such a terribly degraded one that only burnings, etc., will effect

the result of striking terror to the hearts of the evil do-
ers. These people, too, are aghast that more than ten
negro women and children have been lynched during
the past nine months, and that two-thirds of the entire
number lynched were not even charged with this foul
crime. They, too, are more than willing to join with us
in asking as a favor (what is our right as citizens (?) of
our free Republic) that we shall be given a trial by law
for all charges against us, full opportunity in which to
prove our innocence and punishment by law for all
crimes of which the law finds us guilty.

Interviewed by Reporters.

It is not "carrying coals to Newcastle" to tell them
these things, for to them all the facts are received with
the greatest surprise, horror, and indignation. One
woman said she blushed for her race when thinking
of these outrages. Rev. Walter Walsh, to whose congregation of more than a thousand persons I spoke
last night, announced that a perusal of the facts contained in my pamphlet had made him really ill with
horror. There are five daily newspapers in the town,
and every one of them has interviewed me and given
most extended accounts of the meetings. I have been
here four days and have spoken four times. I shall address another meeting to-day and one at the Friends'
meeting-house tomorrow night, and in the afternoon
a drawing-room meeting, cards for which have been
issued by Mrs. Lockhart-Smith, one of the wealthiest
ladies in the town. Her husband is most enthusiastic
over the meetings. When my own country men and
women take hold of the matter in this vigorous way a
means will be found to put down such lawlessness and

free the country from disgrace.

"A Negro Adventuress."

I see the Memphis *Daily Commercial* pays me the compliment of calling me "a negro adventuress," and violently abuses the English people for listening to me. If I am become an adventuress for simply stating facts when invited to do so, by what name must be characterized those who furnish these facts, and those who give the encouragement of their silence? However revolting these lynchings, I did not commit a single one of them, nor could the wildest effort of my imagination manufacture one to equal the reality. If the same zeal to excuse and conceal the facts were exercised to put a stop to these lynchings there would be no need for me to relate and none for the English people to give ear to these tales of barbarity. If the South would throw as much energy into an effort to secure justice to the negro as she has expended in preventing him from obtaining it all these years – if the North would spend as much time in an unequivocal and unceasing demand for justice for him as it has in compromising and condoning wrong against him – the problem would soon be solved. Will it do so? Eight millions of so-called free men and women await the answer, and England waits with them.

IDA B. WELLS.

IDA B. WELLS ABROAD.

Ellen Richardson, the Benefactress of Fred Douglass.

CASTE BASED ON COLOR.

Meeting of the National Baptist Union in London.

Dr. John Clifford and Rev. John F. Aked Are Vehement in Their Denunciations of Lynch Law.

LONDON, April 28.* – *Special Correspondence.* – In Newcastle there lives an old Quaker lady named Ellen Richardson, who was well known to the old Abolishionists for her sympathy and practical help to the cause. She was head mistress of a girls' school back in the 40s when Frederick Douglass first came to Newcastle a fugitive slave. Like most British people, her heart went out in intense sympathy for him away from wife and children, and fearing to return to free (?) America. The fugitive slave law was in force by the consent of the nation, and he was an exile. All Britain sympathized with him, but it was through Ellen Richardson's inspiration that he became free. In a visit to her the day before I left Newcastle she told me how she came to do it. The privilege of an interview was a rare one, as

Miss Richardson is nearly 85 years of age, her hearing is impaired, her health poor, and she rarely sees visitors at all, but I spent nearly the whole of the morning with her. She said that Mr. Douglass, her brother, and herself were at the seaside; that while sitting on the sand together, listening to the fugitive slave's talk, she suddenly asked him: "Frederic would you like to go back to America?" Of course his reply was in the affirmative. Like a flash the inspiration came to her, "Why not buy his freedom!"

John Bright Aided Douglass.

She said nothing of this thought to him, because she knew he belonged to the Garrisonian party, which refused to recognize man's right to barter in human flesh, and that dearly as he might wish to be free, he could not concede to the principle. But the idea had taken possession of her, and being entirely ignorant of how to proceed she consulted a lawyer friend, who told her that as a means to an end so noble he thought there could be no objection to buying a human being. Strengthened by this opinion, without saying a word to her relatives, she wrote letters to different influential persons throughout the kingdom and the responses were many and prompt. She was only a school mistress in moderate circumstances and was not able to advance the sum herself. A letter from John Bright, containing a check for £50, was especially reassuring. She thought what John Bright approved could not be wrong. Not until she had received many subscriptions did she venture to reveal the secret to her own sister and tell her of her difficulty. She knew no way of communicating with Mr. Douglass' whilom master, and she could not tell him her reasons for wishing to know even could he have told her. It so happened that her sister's husband was then in correspondence with a Philadelphia lawyer, and her sister not only approved the plan but entered into enthusiastic correspondence with him.

Ellen Richardson's Noble Work.

Mr. Hugh Auld was approached and found very willing to take English gold for the runaway slave, the sum was named ($800 I believe it was), paid over to him, the free papers were made out, sent to England, and Miss Richardson still preserves them.

Mr. Douglass had all along asserted his right to be free, which theoretically he was, but practically he was still liable to be dragged back into slavery once he left the freedom of Great Britain; so when the good news was told him that he was free indeed he was only told that it was through the generosity of the English friends. He was also given some hundreds of pounds, which he used to establish *Fred Douglass' Paper*, which struck such hard blows against slavery for so long a time after. So modest was Miss Richardson that not until years after the emancipation, when Mr. Douglass was again on a visit to this country, did he know to whom he was most indebted for his freedom. In the same way she was instrumental in purchasing the freedom of Dr. William Wells Brown, who died some years ago in Boston. No mother could be prouder of her child than Miss Richardson is of Mr. Douglass and his achievements, and nearly her whole conversation was about him. She, like other British people who have talked over the matter, cannot understand how the American government could ignore such a man in the World's Fair commission.

Douglass Ignored by the Lady Managers.

They take the ground that such a man, a product of American civilization, was a more wonderful tribute to America's greatness than all the material exhibits stored in the White City, and are perfectly amazed that, commissioner though he was representing Hayti at the World's Fair, the Board of Lady Managers, at their numberless receptions, soirees, etc., made Mr. Douglass the single exception when inviting American and foreign commissions. This caste, based on color, is so entirely foreign to them, "and coming from America, which is always boasting so loudly of her democracy," said one, "it is especially absurd." The negro still hopes that some day the United States will become as great intellectually and morally as she is materially, to protect and honor all her citizens regardless of "race, color, or previous condition," and thus make her professions a living reality.

Rev. Charles F. Aked's Speech.

The National Baptist Union holds its yearly meetings in London every year. This organization is composed of the leading Baptist ministers and laymen of the kingdom, and there were over 500 delegates to the meeting which has just closed. Notice had been published in all the papers that a resolution against lynching would be offered, and I was telegraphed to be present to reply to any questions which might be asked. This was done because at the Unitarian conference at Manchester two weeks ago a similar resolution was defeated because Dr. Brooke Herford had said it was a "terrible misrepresentation" to say the press and pulpit of the South encouraged lynching. Owing to a previous engagement in Bristol I could not be at that conference, but it was thought better that I should cancel other engagements in the north of England and be in London to rebut similar influences. But I was not needed. There was not a single objection expressed or dissentient vote. Rev. Charles F. Aked, the mover of the resolution, had the utterances of Bishops Fitzgerald and Haygood on the subject in which they excused and condoned lynching on the ground of defending the honor of white women.

Bishop Haygood on Lynching.

No other construction can be placed on Bishop Haygood's article in the *Forum* of last October, in which he vigorously condemns lynching in one breath, and with the next, quotes Dr. Hoss' "belief" that 300 white women had been assaulted by colored men, and adds his "opinion" that "this is an underestimate." No mob would wish greater encouragement than this statement, based solely on beliefs and opinions. Mr. Aked also had the New York *Independent* of Feb. 1 containing Rev. J. C. Galloway's encouragement to the same effect, who is a South Carolina minister, as well as that of Dr. Hoss, who has a similar statement in the same number of that excellent journal, and he is a Nashville doctor of divinity and editor of a great church organ.

Clippings from the daily papers of Memphis and Nashville, Tenn., Atlanta, Ga., New Orleans, Paris and Dallas, Texas, where, in many cases, the mob was influenced by the editorials and reports to do these deeds of violence, he had in great number. It was only the rare exception that a Southern or Northern paper had taken an uncompromising stand for the exercise of law, no matter what the crime charged. Where they had failed to do this it was an encouragement to mobs; as for the churches, had there not been the above quotations to use, their very silence in the face of the hanging, shooting, and burning, which are of weekly occurrence, is an encouragement.

An Appeal to the American Church.

Mr. Aked had also the published tabulated list of the Chicago *Tribune* for Jan. 1, 1894, where it was shown, despite Bishop Haygood's "opinion" to the contrary, that only forty of the 158 negroes lynched last year were even charged with outrage upon white women. Mr. Aked was received with great applause, and in a thrilling, eager, impassioned voice began with a statement of the negro's progress, then touched with regret upon the practices of the American people, whose genius he admired, and urged the necessity of the Christian church to do what it could in an appeal to the conscience of the American church to put down this great evil. It was an eloquent speech, a noble effort, and a brave thing to do to champion the cause of the weak and defenseless. He is, as I stated in the former letter, the young and popular minister of Pembroke Chapel, Liverpool, in whose church I made my first address on coming to this country. The shocking lynching of C.J. Miller, which occurred while he was in Chicago last year, made a lasting impression on his mind, and put the first check on his intense admiration for American institutions.

Dr. John Clifford.

Mr. Aked's speech carried weight with it, and the effect might have been credited to his oratorical powers and his impetuosity set down to the ardor and fire of youth; but the man who rose to second the resolution was his very opposite in all these respects. Dr. John Clifford is 58 years of age, of magnificent scholarship, a judicial mind, and the strongest individual influence in London today. After Spurgeon, he was considered the greatest of living Baptists; now that Spurgeon is dead, he occupies first place in the love of his denomination, the people of London, and the country abroad. He has one of the largest and most active churches today at Westbourne Park Chapel, and he is the head of the Polytechnic Institute, which has a membership of over 15,000 young men and women. He is an M.A., L.L.B., and a D. D., all rolled into one, yet he is the most unassuming and lovable of men. The knowledge that Dr. Clifford approves a movement is an earnest of its success. When, therefore, he rose to second the resolution and in calm, dispassionate language pointed out the duties of the churches toward each other, and the conviction that their American brethren only needed encouragement to speak out on this great wrong, and continue speaking till it was put down, his indorsement was greeted with applause, and the resolution was unanimously carried.

Resolution Condemning Lynching Passed.

A feeble brother who declared he traveled with Mr. Douglass through this country nearly fifty years ago, stayed the putting of the resolution to express his approval of the step taken by the Baptist Union and express the hope that the National Baptist Association of America would not only pass a similar resolution, but work to have lynching become a thing of the past. There was a fervent amen to that from one person at least, who shall be nameless. All the London dailies published the resolution, together with the *Christian World, Review of the Churches,* and the Baptist organ, the *Freeman.*

The *Daily Chronicle* had also an admirable leader in commendation of the union's action, and has honored me with a lengthy interview which appears today.

I am to speak in Dr. Clifford's Church Sunday night, and hope to write next time of that great place and the great congregation of a great man and greater preacher.

IDA B. WELLS.

IDA B. WELLS ABROAD.

In the Midst of the Modern Babylon – London.

MANY MAY MEETINGS.

Woman Suffrage the Question of the Day.

Lectures on "Lynching in America"
Meet with Sympathetic and Interested Audiences.

LONDON. May 6.* – *Special Correspondence.* – Whatever the modern Babylon may be in other respects, its Sundays are the wonders of the world and the pride of Christianity. In almost every other city in England the mail is delivered and collected on the Sabbath day. There is no mail delivery on Sunday in London, and no letters are collected from the boxes till 1 a. m. on Monday. There are no newspapers on Sunday – none of consequence – and the few local sheets which are published are not very well patronized. None of the great dailies are published on Sunday. The shops are all closed, except here and there a stall for the sale of the few papers which are printed, and I heard a pious Christian lady criticising severely the innovation of a few shopkeepers who leave the blinds of their windows down on Sunday and their wares displayed with price ticket attached. Unlike Scotland, the omnibuses and street cars and underground railway trains do run here on Sunday. The people have only this one day in which to get a breath of fresh air, and the distances are too great to get out on the heaths and downs otherwise. But the travel is very light, comparatively speaking, not only on these but on the railways as well. The trains are slow and very unsatisfactory; every effort is made to discourage Sunday traveling and make it literally a day of rest.

How Sunday Is Observed Abroad.

The Englishman goes to church or for a walk, or remains decorously at home and respects English observance of Sunday. It is said by those who profess to know that the Englishman in Paris goes to the theaters, cafes, pleasure gardens, and for drives along the Bois de Boulogne and Champs Elysees with the Parisians, and seemingly enjoys the continental Sunday as much as the gay Parisian; that in Spain he is a regular patron of the Sunday bull fights and enters with as keen zest into the sport (?); and that in the United States he reads the Sunday newspaper with as much avidity as the native American. Be that as it may, the uniform observance of the Sabbath day in the British capital, the largest city in the world, is a striking testimony to the Christian and moral sentiment of the British people. This is due in great part to the influence of the Church of England, the active work of leading Christian ministers of the large non-conformist congregations, and the moral stimulus of the May meetings.

May Meetings in London.

May 9 the May meeting as an institution flourishes here as in no other country in the world. For over two centuries the Britisher has been in the habit of coming to London in May to hold annual meetings of all sort. Every Christian denomination, missionary society, philanthropic, moral, social, or political movement in the kingdom which has attained any sort of national prominence, has held or will hold meetings here during this month. It is the one opportunity the country minister and delegate have to combine business with pleasure, and they bring wife and daughter along to see the sights between the meetings. It is also the season with the great social world, and the aristocracy of the kingdom is domiciled in town houses. London is in its glory, the streets are more than crowded, and between the Queen's drawing-rooms, the May meetings and countless receptions, public and private, the scene is indeed a busy one.

The Numerous Societies.

The most prominent of those which have yet been held are the Baptist Union, the Presbyterian and the Protestant Alliance. The Congregational Union is in session this week, also the British Women's Temperance Association and the Women's National Liberal Association, and the Women's Total Abstinence Society. The Women's Liberal Federation held its annual meeting last week.

This is a political organization of women, which sprang, Minerva-like, full-fledged from the brain of Jove, who, in this instance, was Mr. Gladstone. Women had taken no part in politics as a body till the defeat of Mr. Gladstone in 1886. At his suggestion the women of the Liberal party all over the kingdom organized almost immediately, and rallied to his support and won the victory for Liberalism in the next election. Mrs. Gladstone was its first president, then the Countess of Aberdeen, and now the Countess of Carlisle is the presiding officer. After so great a victory for the Liberal party these women saw no reason why they might not win victories for themselves, so they held a national meeting three years ago to discuss that point. There were many who were quite willing to be the reserve force of the great Liberal army represented by the men, and content to help them on to victory, but the great majority wanted the right of suffrage for themselves.

They Demand Woman Suffrage.

They hold that the most direct way to secure the passage of temperance laws, bills making employers liable for accidents to working classes, the eight-hour law, laws for the suppression of vice and to secure home rule for Ireland, is to have the vote themselves, and so they are open and uncompromising in their demand for woman suffrage. Upon this point the conservative element of this powerful woman organization would not agree, and, being in the minority, withdrew and formed a separate organization known as the Woman's Liberal Association. Their president is Lady Fry and they are in session this week. Barring woman suffrage, their work is identical with that of the Woman's Liberal Federation of last week. At their initial reception to delegates at the palatial home of Mrs. Huntington, Monday night, their speeches were identical with those of the meeting last week in condemning the House of

Lords, in advocacy of home rule for Ireland, for the direct veto bill, etc. They profess to believe they can more quickly secure these things by working through the legislative representatives they have than in trying to become members of Parliament themselves.

Provided with Men Expounders.

There is one other difference in their programme: they have prominent men, mostly members of Parliament, to expound these great questions to them, whereas the Federation discussed for themselves and a man speaker was the exception. Yesterday morning Ireland was the subject under discussion, and Mr. John Dillion, M.P., Mr. M.M. Bodkin, M.P., and Michael Davitt were the speakers. In the afternoon local government was the subject. Mrs. Bryce, wife of the man who wrote the "American Commonwealth," presided. This subject was introduced by the Under Secretary of State, Mr. G. W. E. Russell, and by Mr. Graham Wallas, and two ladies who were members each of the school board and town commission. Today "Labor" was the subject, and Mr. Sydney Buxton, the Under Secretary of the Colonies; Mr. Thomas Burt, Secretary to Board of Trade, and Mr. Samuel Woods, vice president of the Miners' Federation – all members of Parliament – enlightened the benighted understanding of the Women's National Liberal Association. The agenda adds that "in the treatment of the above subjects the recent conduct of the House of Lords in rejecting and mutilating liberal measures will be emphasized and at the close of the third session an appropriate resolution will be proposed by Sir Arthur Hayter, Baronet, M. P."

The Countess of Carlisle.

The only difference between these two bodies is whether women shall represent themselves or be represented by men. For my own part I thoroughly enjoyed the wise, dignified, parliamentary presidency of the Countess of Carlisle last week; the splendid speeches, self-possessed, skillful address and witty sallies at the men by the women of the federation, all classes of whom were represented and spoke for themselves. On both sides are women of title, culture, and wealth, but the large number of women who were at Mrs. Huntington's "at home" Monday evening and Mrs. Bryce's brilliant reception last night are social leaders, and as such they best shine. The gorgeous costumes, blazing diamonds, general small talk, social prestige and gracious, high-bred bearing are still to them the first absorptions of women. It is a splendid school from which to graduate into the stronger, more vigorous and active federation. For here, too, are women of wealth, culture, and title, who are devoting their attention to the earnest work of uplifting humanity and cultivating the noblest and best in the masses as well as in the classes.

Some Distinguished Women.

Their costumes were none the less beautiful at their last week's reception, but there was a soul in the countenance born of love for humanity which beautified even the plainest. Here are to be found Lady Henry Somerset, the great temperance leader; Mrs. Hugh Price Hughes, wife of the great Methodist minister; Mrs. Jacob Bright, sister-in-law of John Bright; Mrs. Ormiston Chant, one of the most brilliant platform speakers; Mrs. Sheldon Amos, the writer, and Mrs. Eva

McLaren, the great parliamentarian. She knows more about parliamentary law than the typical society woman does about fashions. Both these bodies were especially kind to me and in thorough sympathy with my work, but the enormous pressure of work consumed all the time, and not a moment was left in which to pass a resolution; though the executive recommended it in each case. At the British Women's Temperance Association tomorrow I am to speak, and the resolution will be passed. I have seen Miss Willard and talked with her, and she sees the subject of lynching as she never saw it before, because she, like others, made the mistake of judging the negro by what his accusers say of him and without hearing his side of the story.

English More Sympathetic than Americans.

Since I have been in London I have had an interview with Dr. Herford, and found out he knows nothing about the South having only been through on a visit; he acknowledged also that he never saw Southern papers, while I had numbers of them. So convinced is he of the injustice he has done the cause he will himself offer the resolution at his conference in this city next Tuesday, and I am to speak in his church Sunday night, where a resolution will also be passed by the congregation!

It is singular that the only opposition I have met has been from Americans, or those who have lived long in America. The Englishman listens "with incredulity until he is convinced that the things I tell are facts; he cannot at first believe that citizens of free (?) America practice and permit such atrocities. But once he is convinced, his condemnation is strong. The American admits the facts, but stubbornly insists on justifying them, and when he can do nothing else asserts that the number is exaggerated.

The Economy of Truth.

Since April 21 the American dispatches report twelve negroes killed. Three in Birmingham, Ala., charged with burning a barn a year ago, and the report tells how ropes were tied round their necks and they were forced to jump off the bridge; eight near Madison, La., charged with murdering the white owner of the plantation, and one burned to death in Arkansas May 2 for the crime (?) of having smallpox. None of these were charged with the foul crime against white women, which the white Americans falsely assert as the cause of lynching, and since it is the white man's newspaper which prints the accounts and the white man's cable which brings them to this country the charge of exaggeration hardly holds good. But anything, however illogical or false, is resorted to by the American tourist to throw disbelief on the story. I have been perfectly amazed at what I heard characterized the other day at the Women's Liberal Federation as the economy of truth exercised by American Christian ministers in discussing this subject. Because they have affected to ignore the question all along is why the mob has grown so bold. But the impartial mind on this side [of] the water hears both sides, "accepts that which facts and reason approve, and rejects that which is contrary to both."

A Fiery Tempered American Woman.

I spoke in Dr. Clifford's church Sunday night week

to an immense audience of 2,000 persons. The good doctor preached a sermon of especial application to my subject then announced that I would speak after the closing hymn and benediction; those who wished to retire would please do so while the last hymn was being sung. Not more than a dozen persons left, and the others sat for three-quarters of an hour longer. They, too, passed a resolution. At the close of the meeting an American woman and her Welsh husband came forward and, in the most excited manner and violent language, denounced my statement that Southern Christians closed their church doors against negroes; they claimed to have seen negroes in white churches in Atlanta, Ga. "If you did," I replied, "it was in the rear seats or the gallery, where they would contaminate none of the white Christians." But they held to it that my statement was impeached and added that they didn't believe that the mayor of Paris, Texas, gave the school children a holiday to see the burning of that negro. I pointed out that their belief did not impeach the facts, and offered to show them all the proofs they wished if they came to my hotel. But they didn't want facts; they didn't deny the burning or other lynchings, but these minor matters called for much talk on their part. They did not see that their rudeness and ill-breeding toward me was a better illustration of all I had said as to the treatment of the negro by the white Christians than words of mine had been.

An Enthusiastic Boy Audience.

Dr. Clifford, who announced that my subject was one he regarded as a matter of supreme importance quietly remarked that he could believe all I said and more. For he had been mortified by expressions from American preachers, who had come over here regarding the negro.

Two weeks from Sunday I am to speak at the church of Moncure D. Conway. He has called on me and is eager that I shall have every opportunity for speech. I spoke before the Protestant Alliance Monday and at a large boy's school yesterday. The head master said he never knew them to be so vociferous in their reception of a speaker before, and when I finished those 300 boys, ranging in age from 10 years old upward to 20, gave me my first specimen of the strength of lungs possessed by English schoolboys. The "three cheers and a tiger Miss Wells" were given with a heartiness which almost raised the roof.

Interviews by All the Leading Papers.

I have been given a two-column interview and excellent leader in the *Daily Chronicle*, the most influential London daily with the largest circulation; the *Christian World* has had a number of articles and gave me a splendid interview last Thursday.

The Westminster *Gazette*, one of the largest evening dailies, has a two-column interview this week. The *Review of the Churches* for May has a good article on the subject of lynching, entitled, "The Stain of the Republic." The *Contemporary Review* will contain an article in the June number, and also the *Review of Reviews*. The *Labour Leader* also has an interview. Before the month is up I shall have made the round of the journals which influence public thought and opinion. Canon Barker, one of the popular Church of England clergymen, thinks that instead of a drawing-room meeting at Lady

Jeunes', a meeting at the Mansion House, with the Lord Mayor to preside, would be the most effective London meeting we could have. He has promised to speak if it is arranged.

IDA B. WELLS.

IDA B. WELLS ABROAD.

A Breakfast with Members of Parliament.

AT SARAH GRAND'S.

Attitude of the Author of "The Heavenly Twins."

The Campaign Against Lynching and the Men and
Women Engaged in it.

LONDON, June 6.* – *Special Correspondence.* – The
thermometer has been at freezing point several times
the past week in town and there has been frost in the
country. Last May when I was here, everybody said
there had not been such a mild and lovely spring for
twenty years; this time it is said there has not been a
time within memory of the oldest inhabitant when
May was as cold and rainy as now. I fully agree with
the American tourist who, when asked about the English climate, remarked that "they had no climate –
only samples." The only other English thing I do not
like is the railway carriage. They can change the one
if they cannot the other. To me, the narrow railway
compartments, with seats facing each other, knees rub-
bing against those of entire strangers, and being forced

to stare into each other's faces for hours, are almost intolerable and would be quite so, were the English not uniformly so courteous as they are, and the journeys comparatively short. But primitive as are these railway carriages, I as a negro can ride in them free from insult or discrimination on account of color, and that's what I cannot do in many States of my own free (?) America. One other thing about English railways must strike the American traveler, the carefulness with which human life is guarded. The lines of railway are carefully inclosed on both sides by stone wall or hedge the entire length, and never cross a roadway as they invariably do in America. The railway always goes under the roadway through a tunnel or over it on a bridge. Passengers are never allowed to cross the track from one side of the station to the other – there is always a bridge or subway. As a consequence accidents to human life are most rare occurrences, and I begin to understand how aghast the Britisher was to see our railway and street car tracks laid through the heart of our towns and cities, and steam engines and cable cars dashing along at the rate of thirty miles per hour. Even in London the only rapid steam or cable locomotion is under ground.

The Story of the Tram.

They call the street cars here tramways, or tram cars, and I puzzled over it very much until I learned that a man named Outram first hit upon the experiment of rolling cars or trucks on tracks – this was before the invention of the steam engine – and all cars so propelled without the aid of steam were called Outram cars. This has since been shortened. The first syllable of the name of the inventor has been dropped, and they are known as trams. I have found many Englishmen who do not know the origin of the word, yet are surprised that the green American does not at first know what he means by trams.

London has been in the throes of a cab strike for two weeks, but beyond making it safe for pedestrians there seems little notice taken of it. The hansom is the only rapid means of general locomotion in London, save the Underground Railway, and there were thousands plying every hour of the day and night. They never slacken the pace when crossing the street, because there are so many streets they would be always stopping. So that between the omnibuses and cabs persons took almost as much risk in crossing the street as they do in Chicago from the cable cars. The strike has taken more than half the usual number of cabs off the streets, and the pedestrian is enjoying the result; for this two-wheeled friend of the weary – the hansom – has rubber tires, and as it rolls along the asphalt pavement there is only the sound of horse's hoofs, and the cab is upon you before you know it.

London is a wonderful city, built as everybody knows in squares – the residence portion of it. The houses are erected generally on the four sides of a hollow square, in which are the trees, seats, grass, and walks of the typical English garden. Only the residents of the square have the entree to this railed-in garden. They have a key to this park in miniature, and walk, play tennis, etc., with their children, or sit under the trees enjoying the fresh air. The passer by has to content himself with the refreshing glimpse of the green grass and inviting shade of those trees which make such a break in the monotony of long rows of brick and stone houses and pavements. The houses are generally ugly, oblong structures of mud-colored brick, perfectly plain and straight the entire height of the three or four stories. This exterior is broken only by the space for windows. The Englishman cares little for outside adornment – it is the interior of his home which he beautifies.

Charms of Antiquity.

There is also the charm of antiquity and historic association about every part of the city. For instance, I am the guest of P. W. Clayden, Esq., editor of the London *Daily News*. His house is near Bloomsbury Square, in the shadow of St. Pancras Church, an old landmark, and from where I am now writing, I look out the windows of the breakfast-room across to Charles Dickens' London home. We are also only a few squares – five minutes' walk – from the British Museum.

I have been too engrossed in the work which brought me here to visit the British museum (although I pass it every day) the Royal Academy, or Westminster Abbey, which every American tourist does visit. I have been to the houses of Parliament twice, and also to Cambridge University. My first visit to the British Parliament was under the escort of Mr. J. Keir Hardie, M. P. Mr. Hardie is a labor member and he outrages all the proprieties by wearing a workman's cap, a dark flannel shirt, and sack coat – the usual workingman's garb – to all the sittings. He is quite a marked contrast to the silk-hatted, frock-coated members by whom he is surrounded. The M. P.'s. sit in Parliament with their hats on, and the sessions are held at night. A great deal of ceremony must be gone through to get a glimpse of the British lawmaking body at work. A card of permit must be issued by a member for admission to the galleries, and it is a mark of honor to be conducted over the building by one. Mr. Hardie himself had to secure a card to permit me to enter the House of Lords, and look upon a lot of real live lords, who, according to the trend of public opinion, should no longer be permitted to sit on their red-feathered sofas and obstruct legislation. There is a special gallery for women, and the night I stood outside the door and peered into the House of Commons I noticed above the speaking chair a wire netting which extended to the ceiling. Behind this were what I took to be gayly dressed wax figures, presumably of historic personages. Imagine my surprise when I was told that this was the ladies' gallery, and it was only behind this cage that they were allowed to appear at all in the sacred precincts hitherto devoted to man.

Ladies in Parliament.

The question of removing the grille was again brought up in Parliament this year, as it has been for several years past, but nothing came of it. An amusing incident happened two weeks ago when two ladies, strangers, had applied for permission to visit the House. A member of Parliament left them, as he thought, at the door while he went into the chamber for the necessary card. Unaware that women were never permitted to enter, and the doorkeeper being for the moment off guard, they followed the member of Parliament up the aisle nearly half way to the speaker's chair, when they were discovered and hurriedly taken out. They are said to be the first ladies who were ever on the floor of the House during a sitting.

Mr. Hardie interviewed me for his paper the *Labor Leader,* and explained much that was strange while we had tea on the beautiful terrace overlooking the Thames at 6 o'clock that evening. British M. P.'s are not paid to legislate and unless they are gentlemen of means they pursue their different avocations meanwhile. An M.P. does not necessarily reside in the district he represents; he may be, and most always is, an entire stranger to his constituents until he "stands" for election. M. P. Naori-ji, a native of India, is representing a London constituency. He is the gentleman about whom Lord Salisbury said: "The time has not come yet for a British constituency to be represented in Parliament by a black man." The English people resented this attempt to draw a color line and promptly returned Naoriji to Parliament, and Lord Rosebery, the present Prime Minister, gave him a dinner on the eve of his election.

My second visit to the House of Commons was purely social, and especially enjoyable because I met again that stanch friend of the colored people, Mr. H. H. Kohlsaat, of Chicago. Mr. William Woodall, M. P., financial secretary to the War Department of her Majesty's government was the host of the occasion and tendered a delightful dinner party to Mr. and Mrs. Kohlsaat, Miss Maud Hambleton, and your humble servant. Beside the host and ourselves there were present Miss Florence Balgarnie, an English speaker and journalist; Mr. Byles, M. P., proprietor of the Bradford *Observer*; Mr. G. W. E. Russell, M. P., a member of the Duke of Bedford's family and an official in the office of the Home Secretary, and Mr. Edmund Robertson, M.P., Civil Lord

of the Admiralty. I have been told that we were specially honored to have as host and fellow guests three
members of Queen Victoria's Cabinet. Mr. and Mrs.
Kohlsaat, their children, and Miss Hambleton left London last week for Paris.

The Agitation Against Lynching.

The agitation against lynching has received fresh
impetus from the reports of the burning alive of the negro who had smallpox in Arkansas and the shameless
way it was confessed by the perpetrators, who have not
yet been punished or even apprehended. Resolutions
against lynchings have been passed by the National
Baptist, Congregational, Unitarian, and temperance
unions at their annual meetings in this city. The Ab-
origines Protection Society passed a similar resolution,
with Lord Northbourne in the chair. I have spoken
before the Protestant Alliance, the Women's Protestant
Union, to the congregations of Bloomsbury Chapel,
Belgravia Congregational Church, and several smaller
congregations. These have all passed strong resolutions and sent them to the American Minister,
Mr. Bayard. I have addressed clubs, drawing-room
meetings, breakfast and dinner parties. I have spoken
not less than thirty-five times at different gatherings
of different sorts during my six weeks' stay in London
and find more and more invitations than I can fill from
people who are anxious to know the facts. Again I cannot help wishing that our own people would give the
same opportunity for open discussion on this subject.
In no other way can it be conquered save to meet it
fairly. At the Democratic Club in this city a most interesting discussion of the subject pro and con took

place. Mr. Herbert Burrows, who took part in the labor congress at Chicago last summer, presided, and the resolution was passed unanimously after I replied to the objectors. The same thing happened at South Place Ethical Institute, where Moncure D. Conway presided. Mr. Conway is a Virginian, who was banished from his home fifty years ago because of his opposition to slavery. He called on me and arranged the details of the meeting at his chapel, and when an American objected to the passage of the resolution Mr. Conway asked his reasons. He produced the utterances of Henry W. Grady, which appeared in the *Century Magazine* some years ago in argument with George W. Cable, in which Mr. Brady was left hors du combat. I happened to know as much about those articles as the reader, and gave Mr. Cable's reply to Mr. Grady's specious arguments.

At the Ideal Club.

At the Ideal Club last Monday night a large and influential concourse gathered for my last London address. Lady Jeune bore the expenses of the meeting, and Mr. Percy Bunting, editor of the *Contemporary Review*, presided. He said that many good people who condemned lynching still felt a delicacy about a public expression of that condemnation on the ground of interference. For his part the cry of humanity knew no such thing as boundary lines; the English people had expressed themselves about Bulgaria, the Siberian convicts, the Russian Jews, and the Armenian Christians. They could, with greater hope of success, appeal to the conscience and humanity of the other great English-speaking race, with which there was a greater bond of union. Miss Frances E. Willard, said he, has come over to teach us how to prosecute temperance work. We have welcomed her with open arms and have been glad of her vigorous blows against drunkenness, and if she had said London contained more drunkenness than any city in the world we would not call it interference. In the same way, he felt sure, there were hundreds of Americans who would not call their protest against the hanging, shooting, and burning alive of human beings interference. Even if they would it would still be the duty of great nations to shame each other, and they were most kind when they pointed out the other's faults. After an address of an hour and a quarter Mr. Alfred Webb, member of Parliament, moved the resolution. He also asked permission to arrange a breakfast for me, to which members of Parliament would be invited, with the hope to hear me. I was only too glad to grant that permission, and this morning at 9:30 o'clock breakfast was served to sixteen members of Parliament, their wives, and one or two other friends.

A Notable Gathering.

Sir Joseph W. Pease was chairman and he occupied himself during breakfast with questioning me as I sat at his right. After his introduction I gave an address of forty minutes and then the great temperance advocate, Sir Wilfrid Lawson, spoke for England, Mr. John Wilson for Scotland, and Mr. Alfred Webb for Ireland, expressing horror of lynching and promising to do all they could to bring influence to bear to have Americans move in this matter. The photograph of the lynching of C. J. Miller, which was reprinted in THE INTER OCEAN last summer and which I have in my possession, went around the beautifully decorated tables as I talked.

Besides the chairman there were four baronets and their wives present. They were filled with amazement and then amusement when I told them that such a gathering for any purpose tendered to a colored person could only happen in monarchical England – that it would be impossible in democratic America.

I am to speak at the Pioneer Club Thursday next and Mrs. Annie Besant will preside. The Pioneer is the first woman's club ever established in London. It has outlived the days of ridicule and most of the brainy women of London belong to it. There is a membership of nearly 500, and the club occupies lovely suites of rooms in Bruton street. They gave a swell reception a few weeks ago, and everybody and her husband, father, brother, or lover was there. The Writers' Club is another woman's organization, and the Princess Christian opened their building a few weeks ago. I spent a most pleasant afternoon there, and, as usual at these gatherings, was talked hoarse on America's lynching and race prejudice. The ubiquitous and (so far as I am concerned) almost invariably rude American was en evidence there. In a strident voice she pronounced my statements false. I found she had never been in the South and was a victim to her own imagination. I heard an English woman remark after the encounter was over that she had seen a side of Mrs. ---- ----'s character which she never knew before.

At Sarah Grand's.

Through the courtesy of a most cultured and charming member of these clubs I was bidden to visit the home of Sarah Grand on her reception day. The author of "The Heavenly Twins" welcomed me most cordially, and, like every one else, made me talk of myself and the treatment of my people when I wished to hear her talk and take observations of the distinguished persons in her drawing-room. There was no chance to get any impressions about her, for she only listened silently and closely, with a quiet question now and again. She is coming to America next year.

But beyond all expectation has been the attention accorded me by the London press. I have quite lost count of the number of times I have been interviewed. The *Daily Chronicle*, the *Daily News*, the *Westminster Gazette*, the *Sun*, the *Star*, and the London *Echo*, all dailies, have devoted columns of space to interviews and a discussion of the subject. The *Labor Leader*, the *Methodist Times*, the *Christian World*, the *Independent*, the *Inquirer*, and the *Westminster Budget*, all weeklies, have had interviews on the same line. The *Review of the Churches* for May, the *Contemporary Review* for June, and the *Review of Reviews* for June, all monthlies have had trenchant articles anent lynching. The *Economist* and the *Spectator* have each more than a column on the subject.

But the closing movement by the London people shows how real their interest, how anxious they are to help the agitation of this subject. At an evening party given by my host last night a committee, including the editors of the daily journals named above, has voluntarily concluded to form a nucleus to aid the work in any way. As an evidence that America is waking up an open letter sent me by the citizens of California, inviting me to come there and lay the subject before the town, was read. And much was said in praise of California's progressive spirit as compared with Boston, New York, and Philadelphia, which are older centers of law and order.

IDA B. WELLS.

IDA B. WELLS ABROAD.

Her Reply to Governor Northen and Others.

THE LYNCHING RECORD.

Effect in England of Abuse by Memphis Papers.

The English Papers and People Resent the Attack on
a Woman.

LONDON, June 23* – *Special Correspondence.* – The seven weeks' agitation in this city against lynch law has waked up the South. Besides Governor Northen's letter of general denial and request that the English people get their facts from a "reputable" source, the Southern press has been very active along the same line. The Memphis *Daily Commercial* exceeds them all in the vigor, vulgarity, and vileness of its attack, not upon lynching, but upon me personally. In its issue of May 26, it devoted nearly four columns to traduction of my personal character, in language more vulgar and obscene than anything the *Police Gazette* ever contained, and wound up all by giving space, for the first time in its history, to an interview with a colored man, J. Thomas Turner, who claimed that "the respect-

85

able colored population of Memphis utterly repudiate Ida Wells and her statements." This is the only reply the *Commercial* can make touching the statements that three respectable colored men were lynched in cold blood in Memphis March 9, 1892; that as the direct result of the *Commercial's* leader and the action of the leading citizens of Memphis, May 25, 1892, my newspaper business was destroyed, my business manager run out of town, and myself threatened with death should I ever return; that on July 22, 1893, a second lynching bee took place on the streets of Memphis with the full knowledge and connivance of the authorities; that the columns of the *Commercial* told how Lee Walker was hanged, half-burned, and then half-grown boys and men dragged his body up Main street and again hanged it before the Courthouse, and that men, women and children stood by and saw the sight; that a telegram was sent from the office of the Board of Trade, ten hours previous to the lynching, apprising THE INTER OCEAN of the fact that the burning would take place and inviting that journal to send me down to write it up.

Statements Not Disproved.

The *Commercial* has not disproved a single one of these statements; it cannot do so. It vainly imagined that a foul tirade against me, and the "repudiation" of a negro sycophant who bent "the pliant hinges of the knee that thrift might follow fawning," would be sufficient refutation of my narration of Memphis' terrible lynching record.

The editors of the *Commercial* have flooded England with copies of that issue, with more detriment to themselves than harm to me. The tone and style of that paper has shocked the English people far more than my own recital could do. It has given then an insight as to the low moral tone of a community that supports a journal which outrages all sense of public decency, that no words of mine could have done. It has brought to the cause warmer friends and stronger supporters than perhaps it might have had.

Since the appearance of that paper in England the Parliamentary breakfast was given me at the Westminster Palace Hotel, and the London anti-lynching committee has been formed. The object of this committee is to aid the ventilation and agitation of the subject, and bring all moral means to bear to assist America to put down lynch law. The Duke of Argyle, whose son is married to one of Queen Victoria's daughters, is a member of the committee. The editors of the *Daily News*, *Echo*, *Chronicle*, and *Westminster Gazette*, Mr. Moncure D. Conway, Rev. C. F. Aked, Mrs. Helen Bright Clark, Miss Kate Ryley, and Mr. Percy Banting, editor of the *Contemporary Review*, are also on the committee. Miss Florence Balgarnie is secretary.

Fell Flat in England.

The London papers would not touch the *Commercial's* article with a pair of tongs. So far as I have been able to learn only one journal to which it was sent, the Liverpool *Daily Post,* has taken any notice of the *Commercial's* foul attack. It its issue of June 13 the *Post* says:

We have received copies of the Memphis *Commercial* of May 26 containing references to Miss Ida B. Wells and her mission. Both the articles are very course in tone and some of the language is such as could not possibly be reproduced in an English journal. Moreover, if we were to convey an idea of the things said we should not only infringe the libel law, but have every reason to believe that we would do a gross and grotesque injustice. Happily it is not necessary for us to consider the element in the Memphis *Commercial's* case to which we have just referred; because whatever that journal might prove against the champion of the colored race would fail altogether to justify the existence of lynch law.

The occurrence of lynching is freely admitted by the Memphis *Commercial*, and is attributed to certain abundant misdemeanors of the black race in the South. We are not encouraged by experience to attach great importance to the accusations of superior races; and we certainly have not been led to believe by history that the men of the Southern States have always proved in their relations with the negroes "the most chivalrous and gentle in the world." A civilized community does not need lynch law, and it is perfectly obvious that a country in which lynch law is resorted to with the approval of public opinion and the concurrence of respectable citizens, as is in the *Commercial* alleged, is one in which any crimes committed by the black race could be effectually dealt with by regular process of law. This is what has been demanded by the large number of representative bodies in this country, which have passed resolutions against the practice of lynching in the Southern States, and this is sufficient reason for their interposition, and the acknowledged existence of lynching is a sufficient justification of the resolutions that have been passed. All else is irrelevant, and we even include under this description a declaration quoted from a colored journalist named Thomas Turner.

The Conditions Do Exist.

It is idle for men to say that the conditions which Miss Wells describes do not exist, when the Memphis *Commercial* admits the existence of lynching, which is the one material accusation of English journalists and English public meetings. Doubtless it is true that many negroes realize that the welfare of the colored race depends almost entirely upon amicable relations with the whites. Moreover, we can well believe "that the right thinking elements of the colored population do not believe that it is right to condone vice in members of their race or justify crimes committed by them." The colored editor asserts that Miss Wells has preached that kind of doctrine. It is absolutely certain that she has not preached that kind of doctrine in this country.

The writer of this editorial, Sir Edward Russell, is one of the leading editors in the kingdom and presided at my Liverpool meeting.

The Liverpool *Weekly Review* adds: "We have recounted the horrors and injustices common to the persecution of the blacks in their naked truth, gleaning them from other authorities than Miss Wells. They constitute a lamentable, sickening list at once a disgrace and a degradation to nineteenth century sense and feeling. Whites of America may not think so; British Christianity does, and, happily, all the scurrility of the American press won't alter the fact."

It is particularly gratifying that, denied any chance to get redress for these gross attacks on my good name at home, such powerful molders of public opinion on this side have come to my defense. I have sent a letter throughout Great Britain in reply, of which the following is an excerpt:

A Woman's Answer.

This is the third time the *Commercial* has so honored me. When a Boston newspaper gave a ten-line leader on the occasion of my visit there, five months after my exile from Memphis, the *Daily Commercial* published a half-column leader of the vilest abuse of the Boston people and myself. When I spoke in Scotland last year and sent the *Commercial* a marked copy of the Aberdeen *Daily Free Press*, containing an account of my address there, again the *Commercial* and other Memphis papers broke forth into foul language concerning me, and sent heavily marked copies to those places. Now, as then, its only reply to my statements about lynching is not proof o' their falsity, but destruction of me personally. This the *Commercial* can safely do. There is no court in the State in which the editor would be punished for these gross libels; and so hardened is the Southern public mind (white) that it does not object to the coarsest language and most obscene vulgarity in its leading journals so long as it is directed against a negro.

No amount of abuse can alter the fact that there respectable colored men were taken out of jail and horribly shot to death in Memphis on March 9, 1892, for firing on white men in self-defense; that the *Daily Commercial's* inflammatory leaders were greatly responsible for that lynching, and the authorities connived at it. Not even the *Commercial* ever charged these men with assaults on white women. The paper openly advised the lynching of the editor of *Free Speech* for protesting against mobs and the false charges brought against their negro victims, and to its utterances on that occasion I owe the destruction of my newspaper and my exile from home.

Can't Change the Record.

All the vile epithets in the vocabulary or reckless statements cannot change the lynching record for 1893. There were lynched in different parts of the State of Tennessee fourteen negroes, three were charged with "assaults on white women," one was lynched "on suspicion," one "by mistake" at Gleason, eight for "murder" and one, Charles Martin, near Memphis for no offense whatever. He failed to stop when ordered to do so by a mob which was hunting another negro, and was shot dead in his tracks. One of the three men who were lynched for nameless crime was only charged with "attempted assault." He jumped in a wagon in which white girls were driving and frightened them. He was caught, put in jail, and the following was sent to THE INTER OCEAN ten hours before the lynching took place: "Lee Walker, colored man, accused of raping white women, in jail here. Will be taken out and burned by whites tonight. Can you send Miss Ida Wells to write it up." Answer. R. M. Martin, with *Public Ledger.*

The *Commercial* and other dailies told in detail on July 23, 1893, how the mob took him from jail, kicked, and cut his flesh with knives, hanged him to a telegraph pole, then placed his corpse on a fire, and men, women, and boys stood by to see it burn; how these half-grown boys dragged the half-charred trunk up the street, and after playing a game of football with it, hanged it again in front of the courthouse, from whence the coroner cut it down, and found the usual verdict.

A Protest.

Even the *Daily Commercial,* which had previously incited mobs, protested against this lynching in these words: "Already the press and pulpit of Britain is thundering at us and Memphis has been held up to them as an illustration of barbarism and savagery, and such scenes as that of last night only tend to confirm such opinion." The editor went on to state that he had heard a young white youth under 17 boast that he had assisted at three "nigger" lynchings, and expected to take part in as many more. This is the *Daily Commercial* of July 23, 1893, after my first tour in England.

The following is from a letter of mine published two weeks ago in THE INTER OCEAN:

"I see the Memphis *Daily Commercial* pays me the compliment of calling me a 'negro adventuress.' If I am become an adventuress for simply stating facts, by what name must be characterized those who furnish these facts? However revolting these lynchings, I did not commit a single one of them, nor could the wildest effort of my imagination manufacture one to equal the reality. If the same zeal to excuse and conceal the facts were exercised to put a stop to these lynchings, there would be no need for me to relate, nor for the English people to give ear to these tales of barbarity. Yours, etc.

"Southport, June 14, 1894. IDA B. WELLS."

Convicted by Their Own Record.

In the same way the other defenders of lynching

in the South have been convicted by their own record. The ink was hardly dry on Governor Northen's letter in the *Daily Chronicle* before the cable brought news of the tarring and feathering of an Englishman in Virginia by a mob, and the hanging and flaying alive of a negro in Governor Northen's own State of Georgia! But there has been no report that Governor Northen has taken steps to punish the perpetrators of that terrible deed. The London *Daily News*, in a ringing leader anent that lynching, pointed out in its issue of June 15 that "the North has not done its duty by its protégés. It freed them and gave them the vote, then failed to protect them in the exercise of their citizenship. These States in which these terrible disorders are common, in which it seems an Englishman is not safe if he offends the mob, are appealing to the world for settlers and capital to develop their magnificent resources. So long as these outrages continue they will appeal in vain. The position of the great body of American people is one of direct responsibility. They are partners with these anarchic States in a great popular government which has hitherto been the admiration and envy of the world. Do they intend to stand by in consenting silence while their flag is dishonored and their government and its institutions disgraced by outrages which bring on all concerned in them the scorn and reprobation of mankind?" Surely with so strong and direct a challenge the American people will bestir themselves to find a remedy for this great wrong and outrage. The *Review of Reviews* for June prints a tabulated synopsis of the lynchings for 1893, and Mr. Stead tersely points out that every other day, except Sunday, last year a negro was lynched, and adds: "This is not civilization; it is savagery."

At Cambridge.

The seven weeks of constant speaking, writing, etc. have forced me to take a rest, and I visited Cambridge University for my first sight-seeing trip. The old historic college buildings, the green trees, and greener meadows were a restful picture, and the visit to Newnham College, the girls' annex, was greatly enjoyed because we had tea with Miss Helen Gladstone, daughter of England's grand old man, who is one of the lady principals of the college. My next privilege was to be the guest of the eldest daughter of John Bright, Mrs. Helen Bright Clark, in her charming home in Somerset. From there I went to Southport, down by the sea, for a visit to Mrs. Thomas Cropper Ryley, the wealthy widow of a man whose name is well known in anti-slavery annals.

Mr. Ryley was one of the faithful few who stood at Henry Ward Beecher's side in 1863, when the mob in Liverpool tried to prevent his being heard on an anti-slavery lecture. In 1866, when Mr. Riley knew that a testimonial was being raised in the United States for Wm. Lloyd Garrison, he undertook the English contribution to that testimonial and collected and forwarded to Jas. Russell Lowell nearly $1,000. Mrs. Ryley and her daughters exhibit among their most precious relics, autograph letters from both Mr. Lowell and Mr. Garrison acknowledging receipt of this money; also a copy of the *Liberator*. Having known and read of these brave anti-slavery workers it is so hard for the English people to believe that for the present emergency no Garrison, Lowell, Phillips, or Beecher responds to the call of duty to rouse the Nation. The Nation and the race needs somebody to say now as Garrison said in August, 1881, in that first copy of the *Liberator*: "I will not equivocate, I will not excuse, I will not retreat a single inch, and I *will be heard*."

Old Abolitionists in Favor.

It is remarkable that those men, who were so hated and persecuted by their own people for taking up an unpopular cause, are the only Americans of that era whose names are known and revered on this side. It is also remarkable that the parents of every American one meets abroad were Abolitionists. It is a passport to favor and consideration which money will not give. Yet it is an especially galling thing to these "children of Abolitionists" to meet the despised negro wherever they turn, and to be forced to be civil to him. The cloven foot shows almost invariably in persons who were never before known to be guilty of a breach of good manners, when the negro question is introduced. A member of Parliament, who took a prominent part in the parliamentary breakfast given me, told me the other day that he dined out that same evening, and took an American lady in to dinner. She was the "daughter of an Abolitionist," and is known to be a woman of culture, refinement, and broad sympathies. Thinking he was sure of his ground he hoped to be able to enlist her sympathies in the negro's cry for justice. He said he was astounded at the bitterness she displayed. "She defended lynching," said he, "and declared that under no circumstances would she eat at table with a negro." He added that he could see more clearly than ever how hard it was for us to be heard in America, if the offspring of the Abolitionists were like that. All this seems passing strange to John Bull, because the

Americans have always boasted of their free country, where there is no class distinction. This crusade is revolutionizing entirely the standards by which American leaders, moral and philanthropic are being judged and many of them will be called on to prove their professions by their work against wrong and outrage upon the negro. Meanwhile the time draws on apace when I shall cease to be a free human being with all the rights and privileges appertaining thereto, and become simply "a colored woman." I am returning to the United States, and in order to make sure I shall not be insulted en route I must avoid taking passage in a ship which is likely to have any considerable number of my countrymen or women as passengers.

IDA B. WELLS.

SELECTED PERSONAL CORRESPONDENCE BETWEEN

IDA B. WELLS & FREDERICK DOUGLASS

The Reason Why Ida B. Wells
Sought Help from Frederick Douglass

While Ida B. Wells was speaking in New York City about the atrocities of lynching in 1892, a British woman named Catherine Impey was in the audience. She was an editor of *Anti-Caste* - a journal that advocated "the brotherhood of mankind irrespective of color or descent." Ms. Impey wrote an account in the journal of a particularly gruesome lynching that took place in Paris, Texas. A Scottish woman named Isabelle Mayo read the story in *Anti-Caste* and was mortified. She arranged to have breakfast with Ms. Impey to find out more information.

When the two ladies met, Ms. Mayo wasn't satisfied with Ms. Impey's explanation about what was taking place in the United States and decided there needed to be someone who could speak to the British

about what was going on. Ms. Impey suggested Ida
B. Wells. Isabelle Mayo offered to provide funding for
Ida's expenses and had the social connections to create
events that would give Ida access to influential people
in the United Kingdom. As a result of their shared interest in fighting for equality of all people, Ms. Impey
and Ms. Mayo joined forces and created the Society for
the Recognition and Brotherhood of Man (SRBM) and
became co-editors of *Anti-Caste*.

When Ida arrived in England in 1893, she was met
by Ms. Impey in Somerset, England. The two traveled
together to Aberdeen, Scotland to meet with Isabelle
Mayo. Three men were living and working with Ms.
Mayo. They were very involved in the preliminary
work to get the speaking tour going; writing letters,
arranging meetings, seeing the press and assembling
mailings.

Early into the speaking tour, Ms. Impey fell in love
with one of the men – Dr. George Ferdinands, who
was a dentist and very dedicated to the cause. He happened to be "Black," from the island of Ceylon (now Sri
Lanka). Ms. Impey sent him a note which expressed
her feelings towards him. For some reason he decided
to show the note to Isabelle Mayo. Despite the fact that
they were working to gain equality for all people, Ms.
Mayo was so outraged by Ms. Impey's behavior that
she called for the ouster of Ms. Impey. She wanted the
Anti-Caste with both of their names to be destroyed,
and for Ida to have nothing to do with Ms. Impey.

Ida didn't see anything wrong with Ms. Impey being attracted to Dr. Ferdinands. In addition, Ms. Impey was the one who originally made it possible for
her to travel to England, so Ida refused to denounce

her. This enraged Ms. Mayo, who decided to with-draw her financial support and her social influence from the scheduled tour. In addition, she implied to others that Ida had come to England uninvited. With funding withdrawn and the SRBM fractured, the tour was cut short, after only a few weeks.

During the next few months, the SRBM did what it could to rebuild and Ida was asked to return to England and resume her speaking. Once Ida arrived in Febru-ary of 1894, she met a young Reverend Charles Aked. Without the social connections of Isabelle Mayo, it was more difficult to have access to influential circles. Rev-erend Aked suggested that Ida obtain a letter from a prominent American who could "vouch" for her anti-lynching work, and thereby secure her legitimacy. Ida wrote letters to Frederick Douglass, who had become her mentor, asking that he "speak to her character."

Seventy-six-year-old Mr. Douglass eventually wrote a letter of recommendation for Ida, which en-abled her to be considered a credible source of infor-mation. Despite Ms. Mayo's obvious intention to cre-ate obstacles for both Ms. Impey and Ida B. Wells, an extensive speaking tour was coordinated.

All of Ida's expenses were paid by the SRBM, but she received almost no pay for the actual work that she did. The modest pay that she received from *The Daily Inter Ocean* newspaper was her main source of income.

The following are a few letters that 32-year-old Ida B. Wells sent to Mr. and Mrs. Douglass, as well as re-sponses from Frederick Douglass. The original letters were handwritten by Ida B. Wells and typed by Fred-erick Douglass. They were reproduced to have a look that is similar to the originals.

Liverpool, Eng.
March 18, 1894
Dear Mr. Douglass,

I arrived safely Friday of last week and
have already addressed an audience of
1500 persons. I find quite to my surprise
that Mrs. Mayo is hostile because I will not
consent to a denunciation of poor Miss
Impey and will therefore have no part
in the work. As Miss Impey is practically
retired because of what I told you; I am
compelled to depend on myself somewhat,
as there are many places where the Brotherhood is not organized. I have come
abroad to give 3 months of my time to
the work and I am going to do it. I shall
make special effort to interview the great
London editors. I am visiting at the
home of Rev. C. H. Aked, the most popular
pastor in Liverpool with the largest congregation. It was at his church I spoke.
He thinks that I should have a letter of
introduction from you.
Please write one as soon as you get this

and forward to me immediately. You know about my work and can the better commend me to these forces than I can speak for myself. Indeed I should be most glad if you will write Mr. Aked himself and thank him in the race's name for the help he has already given the cause. I know you will write the letter at once for me and more than oblige me. It is the second personal favor I ever asked of you, and I would not ask it but that I hope the race will benefit thereby. Please also, do not mention the facts herein mentioned i.e., the disagreement between Miss Impey and Mrs. Mayo and how it leaves me. You know persons are always more apt to draw wrong than right conclusions about anything, so I hope it will remain between us two. Trusting to hear from you soon I remain,
Yours affectionately

Ida B. Wells
53 Bedford Street
Liverpool Eng.

Mr. C. H. Aked is the name of my host, and his address is the same.

P. S. Enclosed in 1893 Sept., 12
Mr. Aked says he had a letter of introduction to you in the states but found you not at home when he called at Anacostia en route home from the Fair. No one told him you were in Chicago until it was too late. He wishes very much that if you do come to England, you will let him know so he may call on you. I enclose his "Personal Notes" so you may see what he says about his trip last summer. He says further that it is very important not only to send me a letter of introduction but if you wish for the splendid success of the work to write letters to all your friends in Great Britain commending me to others. This I know my dear sir you will do and at once as it will take the letters nearly a month to reach here.

Cedar Hill, Anacostia, D. C.
March 27, 1894.

Rev. C. F. Aked,

Dear sir,

Miss Ida B. Wells, now sojourning in England,
known to me by the persecutions to which she has
been subjected on account of her bold exposures and
pungent denunciations of Southern outrages upon
colored people, has told me of the kindness and help
she has received at your hands, at the beginning
of her present mission to England. I join with Miss
Wells in thanking you for opening the doors of your
church, and otherwise assisting her in obtaining a
hearing in England. Once an exile in your land, I
know the value of such help as you have given Miss
Wells. Southern papers have denounced Miss Wells
and have assailed her as an unworthy person, but I
give no credit to their denunciations. The motive for
their assaults is simply to destroy the effect of her
disclosures.
I deem it highly important to the cause of justice

and humanity, that the English people should know the truth concerning the outrages committed upon colored people in the Southern states of our Union. Nations no more than individuals, should live unto themselves. It is the right of each to do what it can to improve the moral sentiment of all. It is well to show the American people that the moral sentiment of our Republic is not the sentiment of England.

The side of the American mob has been told to England by a hundred presses. The side of the negro has been hushed in death. I have tried to speak for the negro in this country and, I hope, not entirely in vain, and I am glad that you now have in England, one so competent as Miss Wells, to tell the negro's side of this story or race persecution.

If I were a few years younger, I would willingly join Miss Wells in her work. You will, I am sure, be glad to know that the Northern people, pulpit and press, are beginning to speak out again[st] the mob, and to doubt the truth of the charge against the negro, by which the mob has sought to justify its savage brutality. I will send you, with this letter, an address on this subject recently delivered in Washington, by myself. It has not been well printed, but

I think it will show you good reasons for doubting the prevalence of the crime now charged against the negro.

I am sorry not to have seen you when you did me the honor to call upon me at my house.

Very truly and gratefully yours,
FREDERICK DOUGLASS.

Cedar Hill, Anacostia, D.C.
March 27th., 1894

Dear Miss Wells,

I am glad to know that you have safely arrived
in England and to see by the papers that you have
already met with friends and have had a hearing in
Liverpool. You are fortunate in having the aid and
support of Mr. Aked, and I will take care to thank
him for his generous action in opening the doors of
his church to you and our cause. I see that you are
already advertised as accredited to England by me.
I had not supposed that, being invited to England,
you needed my endorsement. They who called you
there knew, I suppose, what they were doing and
meant to stand by you and your mission. I do not
see how they could ask you to denounce any one as
a condition of fulfilling the obligation implied in the
invitation given you to come to England. Will you
oblige me by telling me frankly who invited you to
spend three months in England and what assuranc-
es they gave you of support while on this mission? If
they have promised and have failed to perform what
they promised they should be exposed. On the other

hand, if you have not been invited and have gone to England on your own motion and for your own purposes, you ought to have frankly told me so. There is nothing new in the story you now tell me of the attitude of Mrs. Mayo. You told me of her position when you returned from your first visit to England. I am ready to hold up your hands, and want to do so, but I wish to do so intelligently and truthfully.

Very truly yours,
Frederick Douglass

Manchester, April 6th, 1894
Dear Mr. Douglass -

Your letter which I received this morning has hurt me cruelly. With all the discouragements I have received, and the time and money I have sacrificed to the work, I have never felt so like giving up as since I received your very cool and cautious letter this morning, with its tone of distrust and its inference that I have not dealt truthfully with you. The thought never occurred to me that I would need letters of introduction as I was coming as I did before - on invitation. I thought to come here, fill dates made out for me and return home after the work was done. It would have been much easier to secure a letter, had I felt its need when there with you than at this distance. Even after reaching here and finding the situation as it was, I should have tried to do the best I could - but Mr. Aked asked me to write and ask for a letter of introduction simply to have in case there ever was a necessity for it. He gave me a hearing in his church and felt there were others who would do the same thing - without having heard from you - from knowing of me last year. Still he thought it will be fortified. I was so sure that I had only to ask for it to receive it, that I did not hesitate. For without knowing anything about these people and their invitation you *did* know me and had never had cause to doubt my truthfulness. I had never asked favors of you or anyone on personal grounds. The only time before I wrote for the letter was to borrow part of the money to come over on. Even that was to further the cause, for I had been assured of being paid back when I reached here. I am indeed very sorry that you have known me to such little purpose that you must wait to hear from me again before you can send me a simple letter of introduction and recommendation. Even if what I tell you in this letter assures you that you can hold up my hands "intelligently and truthfully," it will be 20 days at least before that letter can reach me, and then it will be too late, for I shall as soon as I finish the dates made for me this month, throw up and come home. My business in Chicago needs me too badly to be giving my time for a work which nobody else will do, and which I cannot afford to do at such cost to myself and suspicion to my friends.

The enclosed letter from Mrs. Mayo will show you that I have <u>not</u> come to England uninvited or on my own notion and for my own purposes. This as you see was written in September and ever since I have been urged by herself as the head of the Scottish Branch of the Society for the Furtherance of the Brotherhood of Man, and Mr. Edwards (who took Miss Impey's place as head of the English Branch) to return. I told them my terms would be my expenses + 2 pounds per week - it was as little as I could come for + then at sacrifice to my business. In November, the Executive Council accepted my terms at a meeting held in Birmingham and promised to advance my passage money when a further meeting was held Jan. 6th on account of bad weather + illness of secretary there was on meeting on that date but he wrote me to come on, as did Mrs. Mayo. Miss Impey, as all understood, was relegated to the background. After I had secured leave of absence and employed someone else on the paper in my place, I had a letter from Mrs. Mayo in December stating that Miss I was still giving trouble and when I came "there must be no secrecy but the whole truth" be told. This was in December. I wrote back immediately saying that I hoped it would not be expected of me to say anything about Miss I - if so, I couldn't come for I would not be a party to further exposure of her weakness. This I wrote to Mr. Edwards + to her. In return I had a letter from the former saying that the Council insisted that I say nothing about Miss I, which accorded with my views. Mrs. Mayo's letter on the other hand said that she thought that my sympathies were all with Miss Impey + while I felt so, she thought I had better not come over, as she would have nothing to do with me if I had anything to do with Miss I. I found this letter in New York when I got there. I wrote immediately to

Mr. Edwards sending her letter and asked him if Mrs. M spoke for the Society + if the Council still expected me to come. He cabled me before sailing to come at once to Liverpool and I did. You asked why I did not tell you the situation - it was because I did not know it myself then. When I got to Liverpool I found that Mrs. M on learning that the Council had sent for me over her letter, resigned her position over it and withdrew her share of the guarantee fund for my expenses and has drawn Scotland after her. Mr. Edwards is so ill, with influenza + rheumatic fever that he cannot attend to the work, and they were depending on the subscriptions at each place to pay expenses. The Council is not a strongly organized body because of the withdrawal of Miss I's friends who feel that she has been ill-treated. In the meantime I am left to my own resources practically, because I will not consent to expose poor Miss I's weakness. For in spite of Mr. Edwards' illness, Mrs. Mayo could + would do the work if I would agree to her plans regarding Miss. I. That I never can or will do even if I must beg my way home. I think if she is in the background she should be permitted to stay there + I should never have consented to come had I known she (Mrs. Mayo) wished me to do this. However, I have found some friends for the cause, who without a single letter of introduction have gone on arranging meetings and getting me chances to be heard in the churches. Of course there is no money in there for me but I welcome gladly every opportunity to spread the truth + shall continue to do so as long as I am here - for since I am here I think it a pity not to utilize the time. Mr. Aked knows the whole story and it was after hearing it that he thought with a letter from you, we could do some good work after all. That is all I wish to do, for I don't want anybody exposed. If they can but pay my expenses, I will give my time as I did before illy* as I can afford it.

I hope I have satisfied you on the points you raise - only let me add that I did not know Mr. Aked had put in the paper that I was accredited to the people of Eng-

*This word is illegible in the original.

land by you - until it appeared. I told
him it was not true altho you knew and
approved my coming. He too felt so sure
that you would send such a letter on demand that he said he knew it to be true
+ therefore used your name. He was the
more anxious to do so because a wealthy
American had asked him in church after
service who I was. I am not to blame for
that; it is too unlike me to sail under false
colors.

I very much regret that the turn of affairs will not permit me to send you the
$25 which I owe you in this letter, but I
hope to have it by the 20th when the note
is due, even if I have to borrow it here.
While my heart bleeds that you should
class me with that large class who have
imposed upon your confidence, I still love
you as the greatest man our race has yet
produced and because of what you have
suffered + endured for the race's sake. I
hope still to be regarded not "My Dear
Miss Wells," but by the name I love to hear
you use - Ida

London - April 26, 1894.

Dear Mrs. Douglass:-

I have just come from Newcastle; where
I saw dear Miss Richardson and had a
long talk with her. She wished me to stay
to tea but I could not so I spent nearly the
whole of one morning with her. Nearly
the whole talk was about "Frederic" and
yourself. I told her how much you longed
to come and see her and thank her in
person for her kindness to Mr. Douglass.
She then told me that Mr. D. had two pho-
tographs of you when he visited her last,
and he gave her one. When he left he
took it to Scotland to show some one and
promised to send her one in return when
he got home. That promise he did not
keep and she says she always blamed him
a little for not sending it. She told me to
tell him so for her, and I told her I knew
you would send her one immediately if
you knew, and that I would tell you, and

that is why I am writing this letter. In further conversation I mentioned that Mr. Douglass had got out a later edition of his life, and she quickly took me up and said she had not seen it. Again I said that Mr. D's time was so taken up with the Fair etc. that he had not time to attend to it, but he would send her one I was very sure and that soon. I know you will be glad to know her thoughts and feelings that [is why] I have written this letter. She is very old - there is no telling when her span of life will close. I thought it best to write now than wait till I saw you again. I hope you are all well and that I may see you again very soon. I shall spend the month of May here, doing what I can, and then in the early part of June will be coming home again. Home did I say? I forgot that I have no home, but back to the "land of the free and home of the brave." With best love to you and Mr. Douglass, I remain

  Yours truly,
    Ida B. Wells

Eaton's Temperance Hotel
22 Guilford St. Russell Sq.
London. May 10th '94

Dear Mr. Douglass,

You will hardly have time to reply to my
last letter before you get this. A matter
of extreme importance comes up since. I
had a talk with Eanon Barker, one of
the popular Church of England clergymen Monday and he says if I have letters
vouching for my testimony and character,
to show that I am speaking for my race
and not myself, from persons of influence
in America, addressed to the Lord Mayor
of London, that a meeting could be arranged in the Mansion House (the Lord
Mayor's residence) to which members of
Parliament and other influential persons
would be invited and that the Lord Mayor
would preside. He would be glad to address the meeting and an expression of
opinion on Lynch Law would go out from

that meeting which would make itself felt in America as nothing said at home has been felt. As you know I have no such letters, but I am extremely anxious that the opportunity shall not be lost, so I come to you again to ask if you will send me a letter addressed to the Lord Mayor of the English people generally or "To whom it may concern" whichever you think best. Mind, I don't ask you to "gush" about me, but for the race's sake I do ask you to speak positively as to my character and the truth of the testimony I bear, and say if I represent the race truly, and not myself alone. You know the history of how I came to be here without such letters; that I came at the invitation of persons who have not kept faith with me etc., but I cannot rehearse all that to mere strangers even if they would listen. What I want is that the people here shall know that 12 negroes have been lynched in the past 2 weeks and nothing is being done about it, and that an expression of opinion from them would have great weight. This they will say if they know I am to be depended upon. I have written Senator Chandler by this same mail. I have told him what I tell you and that I have asked you to call upon him and that you would vouch for my character as I know he will for my facts, for they are the same he used in his speech. If you and he will sign a joint letter, so much the better or if you will write one and he one, whichever you think best. It is an opportunity worth trying for, and I know you my dear Mr. Douglass, will realize its importance and act at once. For if it is to be done at all it must be done quickly, and I have asked Senator Chandler to cable me on receipt of letter whether to expect a letter as I desire or not. This should reach you by May 22 at longest, and I should have a cablegram by 24th, saying if such a letter has been posted and I should get it by June 2nd. Trusting to hear from you soon and favorably, I remain

Yours truly,
Ida B. Wells

Cedar Hill, Anacostia, D. C., May 22, 1894.
Rev. C. F. Aked,

My dear Sir:--
"I believe and therefore speak." Miss Ida B. Wells
is doing a good and much needed work in England
and you are doing noble work in helping her. Humanity is bounded by no geographical or national
lines. Wherever there is oppression, there is the
right and the duty to cry out and cry aloud against
it. But why bring this American question to the attention of England? I will tell you. Because the moral judgment of England is a power and that power
should be employed in the interest of justice. Liberty and humanity, wherever these principles are vio-
lated. There is no breach of friendship in enlisting
the moral influence of one people on the side of the
oppressed and persecuted in a country not our own.
Besides where the voice of the oppressor is heard,
the story of the oppressed should be told. Miss Wells
is a very suitable person to tell it. She does not exag-
gerate. She tells the simple truth and relies upon it
to produce its legitimate effect. A cable gram came
to me a week or two ago, asking if I endorsed Miss
Wells. I gave the answer that I endorsed the mission
of Miss Wells. I do this entirely. I am glad that one
so able and truthful, is in England to tell the negro's

side of this so-called negro problem. The only problem there is in the case, is whether the American people can be brought to deal justly by a people they once held in slavery. It is in fact no negro problem. It is a national problem and it is left to the Christianity of America to solve it. English sentiment and English enlightment can help in this solution as it helped to advance the anti-slavery cause, when slavery existed in our country.

I know of your high standing and influence in England and am glad for my cause sake and for your own sake that you are casting that influence on the right side. By steam and electricity, Liverpool is nearly our next door neighbor. American sentiment on the negro question is very aggressive and has many ways open to entrance into Liverpool and into England. It is very persuasive with all and there is, therefore, good reason to beware of its leaven. As a watchman on the wall, you can warn the people of its wiles.

I am very sorry not to have seen you when you visited the World's Columbian Exposition. Again let me thank you for the general assistance you have rendered to Miss Ida B. Wells.

Very truly and gratefully,

IDA AND I.

Blazing My Own Trail.

GAINING GLOBAL PERSPECTIVE.

From Intimidation to Inspiration.

Feeling Free.

By Michelle Duster

When my great-grandmother, Ida B. Wells, returned from her four-month speaking tour in England, she settled in Chicago in 1894. She married Ferdinand L. Barnett in 1895 and they subsequently had four children within eight years. While raising a growing family, Ida continued her fight for African Americans and women to gain equal treatment as American citizens.

I was born in Chicago in 1963, less than ten miles from where Ida and Ferdinand had lived. I was one of twenty of Ida's great-grandchildren - fifteen of whom were grandchildren of Ida's daughter, Alfreda. As I grew up in a world that afforded me so many rights and opportunities that were denied my ancestors, I had an increasing interest in expressing myself through writing. I joined the high school newspaper staff, as well as that of a city-wide student-run newspaper.

I knew that my great-grandmother had used writing as her weapon to fight against the horrible atrocities that took place during her lifetime. She was one of a small group of African American leaders who fought against enormous odds to impact social change in a country that imposed every barrier imaginable to equal opportunity. During my teenage years my writing recounted what was going on in my high school and to some extent examining other issues such as the 1980 U.S. presidential election.

My interest in writing led well-meaning adults to assume and imply that I wanted to be like my great-grandmother. This comparison was both inspiring and intimidating at the same time. I eventually developed a desire to distance myself from my great-grandmother's incredible precedent. This influenced my decision to leave home in order to experience an environment where no one knew my family history.

Blazing My Own Trail.

The "Black Power" movement of the 1970s was at its height during my teenage years. Affirmative action programs were implemented to correct the historical exclusion of qualified African Americans from schools, housing, businesses and social institutions. In 1981, ninety-eight years after my great-grandmother was refused the right to ride in an equal car on a train, I was one of the African American students who made up approximately eight percent of the student population at an Ivy League institution that had been all-male and overwhelming white for over 200 years.

I was keenly aware that the educational and career opportunities available to me were those that my great-grandmother had fought all of her life for "my people" to enjoy. The opportunity to attend Dartmouth College was not even possible for my mother, let alone my great-grandmother, since the school had been co-ed for a short nine years when I enrolled.

When Ida was my same age of 18, she was living in Holly Springs, Mississippi working as a teacher while supporting her five younger brothers and sisters. She had come of age during the hope and wealth of opportunities available during Reconstruction and was a young adult when the Ku Klux Klan rose and Jim Crow laws came into fruition.

Despite growing hatred and terrorism that targeted the southern Black community in the 1880s, my great-grandmother became part of a small middle class in Memphis. She participated in lyceums at churches where she was surrounded by poetry, literary readings, elocution classes and the bustling exchange of ideas between ex-slaves who had become educated and entered professional careers.

Ten decades later, at the beginning of my college experience, my grandmother Alfreda, (Ida's daughter) wrote a letter to me with advice to stay focused on my studies and not to get involved with student movements on campus. She told me that I should use my typing skills to earn extra money on campus if possible and do what was necessary to graduate.

The longer I was on the campus in the midst of people who came from families with generations of wealth and influence, the less mysterious the elusive world of power, privilege and entitlement became for me. My classmates were ambitious and competitive. There was a focus on being the best, being at the top, and standing out from the competition with the goal of earning top dollars in competitive careers. My fellow classmates and I were told from various sources that we were "Future Leaders of America," so many of us were focused on doing what it took at that time to prepare ourselves to take on the world.

In my classes I sat next to people who were products of the most exclusive, expensive and prestigious high schools in the country. Armed with my Chicago public school education, I was able to earn the same grades as those who grew up with more financial and social privilege. This made me realize that I wasn't a visitor in "their world," but rather an equal participant in "my world."

Despite my grandmother's warnings of not getting involved in activities that would have me labeled as "troublemaker," I couldn't help but be affected by what was going on around me. It was the early 1980s, the beginning of "Reaganomics" and we were still in a "cold war" with Russia. The Berlin Wall was still standing and conservatism was growing.

In my effort to separate myself from my illustrious ancestor, I had become a deejay on the radio rather than join the school newspaper. The radio show that I was part of was constantly under threat to be eliminated, which would have created a void in "urban" music. Some students on campus were demanding that the school divest from South Africa. The all-Black dorm on campus was being threatened to be changed. And there were some individuals on campus who felt the need to be constant sources of insult towards women and minorities. In order to maintain my own sense of dignity, I felt the need to participate in some meetings with fellow minority students and some administrators about the necessity for the concerns of minority students to be addressed.

Even though my fellow classmates and I faced our own set of challenges, I knew that I was fortunate to have so many rights that were unavailable to my ancestors. After all, my great-grandmother was in her late fifties before she had the right to vote. In order to gain social and political voice she had founded the Ida B. Wells Club in 1893.

Ninety years later, I found myself experiencing real efforts to exclude or alienate African Americans, although in less obvious ways than my ancestors had faced. As a double minority in the mountains of Hanover, New Hampshire, away from family and friends, I felt the need to become part of a larger group of African American women. Despite the fact that some women in my family, including my grandmother, were members of Delta Sigma Theta Sorority, Inc., in 1983 I was one of the thirteen women who started a chapter of Alpha Kappa Alpha Sorority, Inc. on Dartmouth's campus.

Gaining Global Perspective.

My grandmother passed away during my sophomore year in college. I was on my way to Mexico for my language abroad program and my parents encouraged me to continue on my trip, rather than change my plans.

For three months I lived with a family in Puebla, Mexico who spoke only Spanish, and I attended school where only Spanish was spoken. The students in the program included 15 men (one of whom was African American), and four women (I was the only African

American) in my group. So there I was in another country, a double minority among my fellow classmates.

I really was interested in learning the culture of Mexico and because of my physical features and the fact that I learned the language pretty well, most people assumed I was Puerto Rican rather than American. I blended in a bit with the culture and was able to see lifestyles, cultural events and historical sites that were completely different than anything accessible in the United States.

One fellow student was from Sri Lanka and another was an Eskimo from Alaska. We became friends and traveled around to different parts of the country (which had very different cultures) to small towns and saw indigenous ceremonies and marketplaces. Outside of major cities we saw some of the archeological sites that included pyramids and other structures built by people who lived centuries before us. In larger cities we saw artwork and met some interesting people, one of whom was the son of José Orozco (world-famous painter) in Guadalajara.

During my travels, I saw for the first time what abject poverty looked like. Once we got outside of the cities, there were communities of people who lived in one-room thatched roof houses with only hammocks and extremely fundamental material possessions. People were still traveling by donkey, had no shoes, running water or any basic amenities that were available even in the poorest neighborhoods in Chicago.

While traveling in Acapulco, a group of us left the beaches and went into the city and stumbled upon a riot that was taking place. I thought of myself as a pho-

130

tojournalist, and tried to get as close as possible to the action to capture something I had never seen before. Graffiti was everywhere, police were everywhere. It was incredible!

I also learned that the Mexicans I had been exposed to while living in Chicago were not the only type of Mexicans. There were huge groups of indigenous people who still lived in Mexico, including Aztecs and Mayans, and Spanish wasn't their native language. They were treated in a discriminatory way within the Mexican society. Most were domestics or worked in other "low level" jobs and were locked out of the power structure in ways that reminded me of the African American experience in the United States. Seeing another culture that practiced discrimination made me wonder if that type of hierarchy in a society is simply human nature. Was it possible for any society to treat all of their citizens equally?

During my three months in Mexico there was a student protest against the university in Puebla and the students took over the bus system. One day they somehow got the buses and blocked the traffic in the center of the city thereby creating gridlock. For two out of the three months I was there, the city buses didn't run. There were some smaller buses that ran, but they were so crowded that I couldn't tolerate them and chose to walk several miles to and from school each day.

In continuum with the turmoil I witnessed, there was practically no toothpaste available in Mexico because of some embargo on toothpaste tubes. So toothpaste was being sold either in really exclusive hotels at incredibly high premium prices, or was being sold on the "black market." I asked my father to send some toothpaste and he thereby became my Mexican family's hero.

I had two Mexican brothers (Pedro and Geraldo) and one sister (Norma). Geraldo was in dental school at the time. My Mexican sister, Norma, didn't have much freedom compared to most Americans I knew. She had to be accompanied most places by either her brothers or father. It made me realize by contrast, how much freedom, I as an American female had.

Inflation was outrageous during my short time living in the country. I saw the prices of things like gas rise at least 400 percent. There were long lines for everything and it was pretty well known that bribery was a way to get things done. I learned how the art of corruption, barter and negotiation worked and realized that despite the problems in the United States, at least there were some laws that made things more possible for the "average" person to have a chance.

While in Mexico, I saw the 1983 election victory of Harold Washington for Mayor of Chicago. It was fascinating to see his historic win relayed all in Spanish in another country. My Mexican brother Pedro and I had a long discussion about race relations in the United States and it was interesting to me to learn how much awareness he had about the fact that African Americans had been oppressed. He was very familiar with Martin Luther King, Jr. and Malcolm X and told me that most people in Mexico look at African Americans more as their brothers and sisters, versus how they regard Caucasians. His statement made me realize that in some ways I was more accepted in Mexico than I was in some areas of my own country.

When I returned to the United States, I learned that

a friend of mine was going to participate in a program in Scotland for her philosophy major. She and a fellow classmate were planning to travel around Europe for a month before the start of her program. I decided to join them because it seemed like it would be difficult to have the time to do something like that once I started working in the "real world."

The three of us - two African American women and one Asian American woman - got a *Let's Go Europe* book, youth hostel cards and Eurail passes so we could take the trains throughout Europe. We flew from New York City to London with no specific plan of where we would go or how long we would stay after that.

We spent two days in London before moving on to see as much of Europe in 30 days as possible. What I remember most about London was seeing the changing of the guard at Buckingham Palace and marveling at how small the cars were. We went on to visit Switzerland (Geneva and Lugano); Austria (Innsbruck and Vienna); Italy (Florence, Rome, Pisa and Venice); Germany (Frankfurt and Munich); Zagreb, Yugoslavia; Paris, France; and I took a detour by myself and stopped in Strasbourg, France to visit my French sister with whom I had become friends during my language exchange program in France while in high school.

One thing that struck me as particularly interesting about traveling overseas was that most people didn't assume that I was American. People assumed that I was anything from North African (Egyptian, Moroccan, Libyan, or Tunisian), Hispanic, Caribbean or South American. A part of that assumption could be based on the fact that I spoke both Spanish and French. Even when people learned that I was American they insisted that I had to be first generation and my parents were originally from another country. It was incomprehensible to most people that I could be a seventh generation American of African descent who grew up on the South Side of Chicago.

As a result of the experiences in both our neighboring country of Mexico and the numerous countries I visited in Europe, I am convinced that people around the world are more alike than different. I truly feel that I am a citizen of the world, rather than "only" an African American woman. There is a common experience between women of African descent in particular, and all women in general.

During my travels I met many people who truly didn't understand the concept of discrimination based only on race. The more questions they asked me about prejudice towards African Americans, the more difficult it was to explain. These challenging conversations reiterated just how arbitrary and ridiculous it is to treat people differently based only on skin color.

Growing Closer to My Heritage.

A couple of years after I graduated from college, my Aunt Ida (Ida B. Wells' daughter) passed away. My aunt took some of the knowledge about her parents along with her. Because I was craving a place of my own to live, and didn't want to see her co-op apartment sold, I ultimately ended up living in the apartment that my grandmother and aunt had shared for decades. I was very familiar with many of the neighbors, who were my grandmother's generation. I had befriended several of them over the years. Spending time around people in this age group gave me a strong sense of history.

As I listened to the stories of my elders, my desire to document the rich history started to grow. In addition, other people had an increasing desire to learn and document information about the life and times of my great-grandmother. I was in graduate school in Chicago studying film production when a documentary filmmaker contacted our family about a film he was producing about Ida B. Wells. I had the opportunity to work with the producer as an assistant. This experience helped me learn more about my own family as well as how a professional film was made.

While working on the film, *Ida B. Wells: A Passion for Justice*, I came in contact with historians and scholars who knew more specific information regarding some parts of my great-grandmother's life than I did. They had studied her work and times in which she lived in detail, whereas I had anecdotal information. I gained scholarly insight from people who weren't part of my family.

I learned more detailed information about the social dynamics that shaped Ida's life, which paralleled the history of this country. This experience made me want to delve deeper into exploring and exposing the ways that African Americans had overcome the systemic racism that prevailed in our country. I wanted to be involved with projects that highlighted the achievements of African Americans. This interest took me to New York City.

Exposure to the Greats of My Time.

While a lot of my friends were getting married and starting families, I was living in New York City trying to find my place in the world of highlighting the achievements of African Americans. I got involved in producing music concerts and special events that featured some well-known performers, writers and scholars of my time. I had the opportunity to meet Billy Dee Williams, Maya Angelou, Kwame Ture (formerly Stokely Carmichael), Cornel West, Paula J. Giddings, B. B. King, Sidney Poitier, Nancy Wilson, Ed Bradley, Phyllis Hyman, Toni Morrison, Lena Horne, Max Roach, Harry Belafonte, Louis Gossett, Jr., and many other talented and inspiring people.

Part of my job was to write scripts for slide shows and hosts of award shows. I also wrote and was involved with design and production of program books. At the events, I was the one behind the stage or on the side who was coordinating the efforts of numerous people who made the event run smoothly.

I think having the chance to work in this world and come in contact with these historymakers further demystified the aura of fame and fortune for me. Many of the people I came in contact with were extremely friendly, welcoming and encouraging. Interacting with them made me feel that I could someday make my contribution to this world. It made the legacy of Ida B. Wells less intimidating because for the first time I was able to imagine her as a "real" person, rather than a larger-than-life figure whose shoes some people thought I could fill.

From Intimidation to Inspiration.

As I headed into my late thirties and early forties, my ability to define myself within and outside of my family legacy strengthened. I became comfortable enough to learn about Ida's life and delve into her work without feeling pressure to measure up to what she achieved. She became inspiring to me as a woman, rather than an intimidating historical figure. As a result of my quest to become more knowledgeable about my great-grandmother and the women who lived during her time, I marvel at their bravery. Their strength in the face of unthinkable oppression gives me inspiration to feel that I can handle anything that comes my way.

Maybe because Ida was obviously an independent woman, in addition to being a writer, my curiosity has increased regarding how she handled going against the "norm." I have learned quite a bit about her accomplishments, challenges and circumstances. Some of the scholars I met in 1989 while working on the documentary film, *Ida B. Wells: A Passion for Justice*, told me that they saw similarities between Ida and me. This notion was dismissed by me because three generations separated us – after all, she died thirty-two years before I was born. Only through her writings have I had an opportunity to get a sense of how she actually viewed the world.

As I have strained to read the original newspaper articles that she wrote over 115 years ago, I have started to feel a closer connection to this woman whose blood runs through my veins. I am now more than 10 years older than Ida was when she was thrust into a leadership role. At this point I can look back at her with more objectivity and speculate about what helped her become the woman she was. I understand now that circumstances made a huge impact on what happened in Ida's life and she came of age during an incredibly tumultuous time in our country's history.

As I learn more about my great-grandmother, I marvel at the number of similarities between us. I share her unwillingness to be silent about being treated unfairly, her lack of focus on becoming a young wife and mother, as well as her love of travel. Ida got married "late" for her time – close to the age of 33. I have yet to take that path, thereby ensuring that I will also be considered "late" for my time. She and I both lived in New York City exactly one century apart – she for one year in 1892, I for almost ten (during the 1990s). In some ways I feel a friendship with her because she defied the societal expectations and limitations of her day and in my own way it seems I'm doing the same.

In multiple ways I feel that my choices regarding my life go against the majority and I'm blazing my own trail and making up my own rules as I go along. Reading through these articles that Ida wrote in 1894, I am struck by how I am doing some of the same things as she, but under different circumstances for very different reasons.

Ida traveled to the United Kingdom twice during her lifetime in 1893 and 1894. As a single woman in the 1890s, Ida stayed in the homes of private citizens while she was speaking, lecturing, meeting and writing about the atrocities that were taking place in the United States. Her mission was to gain support from the British to denounce the practice of lynching and institute due process of law in the United States. As a single woman in the 1980s I had the freedom and financial means to travel overseas with two other single women to enjoy Europe as a tourist.

In Ida's article, written on June 6, 1894 she wrote:

London is a wonderful city, built as everybody knows in squares – the residence portion of it. The houses are erected generally on the four sides of a hollow square, in which are the trees, seats, grass, and walks of the typical English garden. Only the residents of the square have the entrée to this railed-in garden. They have a key to this park in miniature, and walk, play tennis, etc., with their children, or sit under the trees enjoying the fresh air. The passer by has to content himself with the refreshing glimpse of the green grass and inviting shade of those trees which make such a break in the monotony of long rows of brick and stone houses and pavements. The houses are generally ugly, oblong structures of mud-colored brick, perfectly plain and straight the entire height of the three or four stories. This exterior is broken only by the space for windows. The Englishman cares little for outside adornment – it is the interior of his home which he beautifies. It's almost eerie to read her descriptions of what she saw in London in 1894. Almost ninety years later when I went to London in 1983, I saw some of the same exact things as she.

I traveled to London a second time in 1999 with my two brothers and my father. This time I stayed a week and had the opportunity to visit more places, not just because of time, but also because of money. I wasn't a broke student anymore and could enjoy more experiences. We did the requisite tourist things like have tea at Harrods, took a tour of the Tower of London where we saw the crown jewels as well as the chambers, rooms and gardens. We went to the Tate Museum, Piccadilly Circus, took a tour on the Thames River and generally walked around and saw as much as possible in five days. We saw Buckingham Palace as well as Kensington Palace where the tens of thousands of flowers for

Princess Diana had been laid.

Both times I went to simply enjoy the experience of being in another city in another country. I wasn't fighting for anything. I wasn't representing anything. I wasn't trying to change anyone's mind about anything. I was just Michelle walking around taking pictures of historic sites, trying different foods and interacting with interesting people.

During my trips to London, my impression of the British was one of amazement at the level of civility and patience I saw. Americans in comparison can be impatient and condescending, so I understand where the "Ugly American" reputation comes from. I'll never forget the mounted British police officer in London saying "Move along, please. Step aside, please." It was almost disorienting to me because I couldn't remember ever hearing a police officer saying the word "please" in the United States. In the neighborhoods where I lived in both Chicago and New York very few people I know would describe the police as polite.

Feeling Free.

The United States of America boasts of being a country where "all men are created equal." However, for several centuries after Europeans took control of what has become our country, with a small number of exceptions, only white men could be landowners. Only white men could vote. Only white men could attend certain schools. Only white men would be hired and promoted for certain jobs. And only white men were accepted into certain social and sports clubs.

Within the last century there have been numerous African Americans who experienced more equitable treatment while abroad than they had while "at home" in their native United States of America. In Ida's article from March 24, 1894, she described the feeling of experiencing freedom while in London: *....it is like being born into another world, to be welcomed among persons of the highest order of intellectual and social culture as if one were one of themselves. Here a "colored" person can ride in any sort of conveyance in any part of the country without being insulted, stop at any hotel, or be accommodated at any restaurant one wishes without being refused with contempt; wander into any picture gallery, lecture-room, concert hall, theater, or church and receive only the most courteous treatment from officials and fellow sightseers. The privilege of being once in a country where "man's a man for a' that" is one which can best be appreciated by those Americans whose black skins are a bar to them receiving genuine courtesy and kindliness at home.*

Seventy-six years after Ida died, a brilliant, young, charismatic, African American man with an African name decided to run for the President of the United States. After centuries of people with African blood in their veins being ostracized, ridiculed, humiliated, bought, sold, burned, shot, waterhosed down, arrested, spit on, terrorized and killed, Barack Hussein Obama decided to challenge every notion of our country's past.

I volunteered for the campaign and was really struck by the enthusiasm of some of the 20-something- year-old Caucasian volunteers I encountered. They were so vibrant, enthusiastic, open-minded and excited. It was amazing to see them working hard to help an African American man get elected. Very different than some of the people I encountered while in my twenties.

On August 28, 2008, I stood in Invesco Field in Denver, Colorado at the Democratic National Convention, where Mr. Obama gave his acceptance speech. A rainbow of faces all showing signs of jubilation at the possibilities of what our country could be made me feel that maybe our country was beginning to change.

At the event I attended on election night, November 4, 2008, I got into a conversation with one young Caucasian lady who told me that she couldn't even understand how some people could be shallow enough to not want Barack Obama to be President "just because he was Black." All I could think was "thank God for the younger folks." Maybe we're finally headed towards a world where people will be judged by their talent rather than their physical characteristics.

When the election results were final, I could only think about what my great-grandmother, Ida B. Wells, and all of my other ancestors, would have thought of that unseasonably warm day in Chicago. Hundreds of thousands of people representing a wide variety of ages, religions, ethnicities and sexual orientations gathered in Grant Park to celebrate the historic moment.

I celebrated the inauguration in Washington, DC on January 20, 2009 with a group of friends who attended Dartmouth College. Everyone in my group, as well as millions of people around the country, cried tears of joy and breathed a huge sigh of relief at the reality that "Yes We Can" had turned into "Yes We Did." As I watched the parade on Pennsylvania Avenue for the 44th President of the United States of America I started to feel that all of the millions of people who came before us, who fought, sacrificed and refused to stop dreaming could cautiously begin to rest.

A BIOGRAPHY *of* IDA B. WELLS

BY MICHELLE DUSTER

Ida B. Wells was a fearless journalist, anti-lynching crusader, speaker, suffragist, and women's rights advocate. She stands as one of the nation's most uncompromising leaders and most ardent fighters for justice and equality. She was born a slave in 1862 (three years before slavery ended in 1865), in Holly Springs, Mississippi. She came of age during Reconstruction when there were large numbers of volunteers and substantial resources allocated towards the rebuilding of the South. Schools were established to educate ex-slaves. The newly freed African Americans took advantage of their new rights and enthusiastically exercised their voting privileges, and also became politicians, business owners and land owners.

Ida's father, James, was a carpenter and her mother, Elizabeth, was a famous cook. Ida, who was the oldest of eight children, learned to read at a young age when she attended Shaw University (later called Rust College). She was surrounded by political activists and read the newspaper to her father and his friends, who regularly discussed current events.

In the summer of 1878, Ida was visiting her grand-mother, Peggy Wells' farm in Grenada, Mississippi when tragedy hit. A large-spread epidemic of yellow fever swept through Holly Springs and both of her parents and her infant brother, Stanley, died within days. Another brother, Eddie, had died a few years earlier. Against counsel of all adults in her life, Ida returned to Holly Springs and defied all efforts of well-meaning adults to break up her five remaining siblings in order for them to get care. At the age of 16, she lengthened her skirt, put her hair in a bun in order to look older and secured a job as a teacher.

Ida traveled six miles by mule to the rural school on Sundays and returned to Holly Springs on Fridays. Her grandmother helped with the children during the week for a few months before she suffered a stroke and returned to her farm. After that, a friend of Ida's mother helped for a while. After almost two years of this brutal schedule, Ida finally relented and accepted help from her aunts. Her Aunt Belle took Ida's sister Eugenia (who was crippled) and her two brothers (James and George) to live on her farm. Ida and her two sisters, Annie and Lily, went to Memphis to live with their Aunt Fannie, who was widowed and had three children.

During Reconstruction some African Americans had started to prosper and managed to surpass some white Southerners in their accomplishments. Recon-struction ended in 1877, and a backlash started to swell. Throughout the South legislation was rapidly passed that separated the races in every area of life from cra-dle to grave - even instituting separate cemeteries. In 1881, a new law was passed in Tennessee which indi-cated that Black and white passengers on trains had to be seated in separate cars.

Separate schools based on race were established and the black schools were overcrowded, had very limited supplies and the teachers were underpaid. Shortly after moving, Ida secured a teaching job in Woodstock, Tennessee, about ten miles north of Memphis. She rode the train to and from work on a regular basis. One day in the early 1880s, Ida sat down in the ladies' coach on the Chesapeake, Ohio & Southwestern Railroad as she had on many occasions. In his effort to enforce the new segregation rules, the conductor of the train told her to go to the "colored car," which doubled as the smoking car. Ida refused to leave because she was a lady, and had purchased a ticket for the ladies' coach. According to Ida B. Wells in her autobiography: "[The conductor] tried to drag me out of the seat, but the moment he caught hold of my arm I fastened my teeth in the back of his hand. I had braced my feet against the seat in front and was holding to the back, and as he had already been badly bitten he didn't try it again by himself. He went forward and got the baggageman and another man to help him and of course they succeeded in dragging me out." Once she was forcefully removed from the train all of the white passengers applauded.

The sense of humiliation and indignation that Ida felt after being dragged off the train propelled her to file suit against the railroad company. When she returned to Memphis, she immediately hired an attorney to sue the railroad. She filed a case against the railroad in 1884 and won in the local circuit court, but the railroad company appealed to the Supreme Court of Tennessee, and the lower court's ruling was reversed in April of 1887.*

In the mid-1880s Ida's aunt, cousins and sisters

* The court concluded that there were separate accommodations which were equal in all respects and "it is evident that the purpose of the defendant in error was to harass with a view to this suit, and that her persistence was not in good faith to obtain a comfortable seat for the short ride." *Cases Argued and Determined in the Supreme Court of Tennessee for the Western Division, Jackson, April Term, 1887.* Chesapeake, Ohio & Southwestern Railroad Company v. Wells , p. 491.

moved to California, leaving Ida alone in the bustling city of Memphis. In addition to her teaching job, Ida began to write articles for church newspapers. She insisted on writing articles about politics and social issues, when most women were writing about "women's topics" such as book reviews, school news and articles about marriage and children. Her articles began to be reprinted in other newspapers around the country, which increased her audience and influence. She wrote an article that detailed the incident on the train which made her into a well-known figure in a segment of the Memphis population.

In 1889, Ida was approached to write for the *Free Speech and Headlight* newspaper – a paper which was the result of a merger between the *Free Speech* owned by Reverend Taylor Nightingale, the pastor of Beale Street Baptist Church, and the *Marion Headlight*, published by a journalist named J. L. Fleming. Ida agreed to write for the paper with the insistence that she become equal partner and editor. With her new responsibility, Ida immediately shortened the name of the paper to the Memphis *Free Speech*.

Her writings in the *Free Speech* continued in their fiery style of criticizing injustice wherever she saw it. In 1891, she wrote an article criticizing the Memphis school system for the blatant inequality between the educations available for African American students versus white students in their schools. The article created such an uproar that she lost her teaching job after over ten years in the profession. This left her with no income, so she focused her attention full-time on pursuing her journalism career. Ida traveled tirelessly to communities along the Mississippi River selling subscriptions to the newspaper.

A few months later, in 1892, Ida's good friends,

Thomas Moss, Calvin McDowell, and Will Henry Stewart opened the People's Grocery store, which white business owners viewed as a threat. In March of 1892, Ida was in Natchez, Mississippi selling newspaper subscriptions, when an incident occurred that would change her life forever. In order to eliminate the competition, an attack on the People's Grocery was staged. The African American male store owners fought back, shooting one of the attackers. The three men were arrested and taken to jail. Before a trial ever came to pass, a lynch mob entered the jail and took the men to an open field where they were mutilated, tortured and brutally murdered. The store was then vandalized and destroyed. It was believed that some in the lynch mob were also members of the law enforcement personnel.

There was a deep sense within the African American community that it was impossible to experience justice in the city of Memphis. In response to the murder of her friends, Ida wrote in the *Free Speech* "The city of Memphis has demonstrated that neither character nor standing avails the Negro if he dares to protect himself against the white man or become his rival. There is nothing we can do about the lynching now, as we are out-numbered and without arms. The white mob could help itself to ammunition without pay, but the order is rigidly enforced against the selling of guns to Negroes. There is therefore only one thing left to do; save our money and leave a town which will neither protect our lives and property, nor give us a fair trial in the courts, but takes us out and murders us in cold blood when accused by white persons."

Many people took Ida's advice and moved west to places like Oklahoma, California and Kansas. In her newspaper, Ida encouraged the African Americans who remained in Memphis to boycott white-owned

business and the streetcars. For six weeks people boy-
cotted the streetcars and a superintendent and treasur-
er of the City Railway Company came to her office and
tried to convince her to use her influence to stop the
boycott. She accused the entire white community of
killing her friends, since they had done nothing to stop
the lynchings.

As injustices against former slaves raged throughout the South and a reign of terror continued, Ida's
sense of indignation and quest for justice was fueled.
She started researching the facts behind other lynchings that had taken place. In so many cases the rape
of white women was used as the excuse to murder
African American men, however that wasn't a reflec-
tion of the truth. Ida eventually wrote an article where
she implied that some of the liaisons between Black
men and white women were consensual. She was already in Philadelphia attending a convention of the
African Methodist Episcopal Church when the article
was printed. The article incited the destruction of her
newspaper office and a price was put on her head.

With no money and only the belongings she had
with her, Ida went to New York City and T. Thomas
Fortune offered her the opportunity to work at his *New
York Age* newspaper. Her determination to expose the
facts behind the lawlessness that was raging through
the South led her to hire private investigators to collect
information about the lynchings that took place.

In 1892, she meticulously documented the numbers
and reasons for lynchings and with the financial help
of women in the churches, wrote and published the
pamphlet *Southern Horrors: Lynch Law in All Its Phases*. Through her pamphlet and increasing number of
speaking engagements, Ida hoped to stir social change
from the North. Her efforts didn't elicit the response

she hoped, so when she was asked to travel to the United Kingdom to tell her story she jumped at the opportunity to possibly put international pressure on the United States to put an end to this brutal practice.

Her trip to the England in 1893 further convinced her that people outside of the United States needed to know what was going on, because she found that the information they were being told was incorrect. She strongly believed that if people knew the truth, they would put pressure on the power structure of the country to do something to stop the atrocities.

In keeping with her mission, she partnered with Frederick Douglass to publish a pamphlet, *The Reason Why the Colored American is not in the World's Columbian Exposition*. The goal was to inform foreigners who attended the World's Fair of 1893 in Chicago about the contributions that African Americans had made to the country as well as document the horrible way that the United States treated its own citizens. The two other contributors to the pamphlet were Irvine Garland Penn and Ferdinand L. Barnett.

In 1894, Ida returned to England to continue telling the facts about lynching. When she came back to the United States, she realized she had no place to call "home." A burgeoning attraction between Ida and Ferdinand L. Barnett influenced her decision to return to Chicago. He was a man ten years her senior, an accomplished and well-known attorney, a fellow crusader, as well as the founder and owner of *The Conservator* newspaper. He was a widower, who had two children from his first marriage. Ferdinand L. Barnett and Ida B. Wells wed on June 27, 1895 and had four children of their own in eight years.

Ida wrote: "I was married in the city of Chicago to Attorney F. L. Barnett, and retired to what I thought was the privacy of a home." She did not stay retired long and continued writing and organizing. Ferdinand was a good match for Ida because he encouraged her passion and supported her work. In addition to numerous newspaper articles, she wrote several pamphlets including *A Red Record* in 1895, *Lynch Law in Georgia* in 1899 and *Mob Rule in New Orleans* in 1900.

In 1909, Ida B. Wells-Barnett became one of the founding members of the National Association for the Advancement of Colored People (NAACP). Because of her unwillingness to compromise and determination to accept nothing less than total equality, Ida was viewed as one of the most radical of the so-called "radicals." As a result of her "militant" views, her level of involvement with the organization was limited, and she didn't assume any positions of leadership.

Ever the restless soul, Ida helped develop numerous reform organizations including the Ida B. Wells Club and the Alpha Suffrage Club. She became a tireless worker for women to gain the right to vote. She marched in the famous 1913 march for universal suffrage in Washington, DC. In keeping with her unwillingness to settle for "second class" treatment, she defied the request of the organizers that African American women march in the back of the parade. Instead, she left the line-up and inserted herself in the front with the rest of the Illinois delegates.

Not able to tolerate inequality of any kind, Ida B. Wells-Barnett, along with Jane Addams, successfully blocked the establishment of separation of races in Chicago schools. In 1915, she and the Alpha Suffrage Club helped Oscar DePriest become Chicago's first African American alderman. He went on to be elected to Congress in 1928.

Only ten years after women won the right to vote,

Ida pushed women's rights even further and decided to run for the Illinois State Senate in 1930. She lost the race, but went down in history as one of the first African American women to run for public office in the United States. A year later, on March 25, 1931 she died in Chicago, Illinois a few months before the age of sixty-nine. She left a formidable legacy of undaunted courage and tenacity in the fight against racism and sexism.

Sources for Troy Duster, Ph.D.

Giddings, Paula J., *Ida: A Sword Among Lions: Ida B. Wells and the Campaign Against Lynching,* New York: HarperCollins (Amistad), 2008.

Gusfield, Joseph R., *Symbolic Crusade: Status Politics and the American Temperance Movement.* Westport Conn.: Greenwood Press, 1980.

Hochschild, Adam, *Bury the Chains: Prophets and Rebels in the Fight to Free an Empire's Slaves,* Boston: Houghton Mifflin, 2005.

Sources for Michelle Duster

Davidson, James West, *They Say: Ida B. Wells and the Reconstruction of Race,* New York: Oxford University Press, 2007.

Duster, Alfreda M. (ed), *Crusade for Justice: The Autobiography of Ida B. Wells,* Chicago: University of Chicago Press, 1970.

Fairclough, Adam, *Better Day Coming: Blacks and Equality, 1890-2000,* New York: Viking, 2001. pp. 22-39

Fradin, Dennis Brindell and Fradin, Judith Bloom, *Ida B. Wells: Mother of the Civil Rights Movement,* New York: Clarion Books, 2000.

Giddings, Paula J., *Ida: A Sword Among Lions: Ida B. Wells and the Campaign Against Lynching,* New York: HarperCollins (Amistad), 2008.

Schecter, Patricia A., *Ida B. Wells-Barnett & American Reform 1880-1930,* Chapel Hill and London: The University of North Carolina Press, 2001.

153

Archives

Regenstein Library, University of Chicago,
Chicago, Illinois
Ida B. Wells Papers

The Chicago History Museum, Chicago, Illinois

Library of Congress, Washington, DC
Frederick Douglass Papers

Acknowledgements
from Michelle Duster

My cousin, Charles E. Duster, Jr. is a meticulous researcher and a joy to work with. There is no way this project could have been done as easily without his extensive assistance. He and I worked tirelessly to reconstruct and ultimately reproduce these articles and letters to make them as true to the way they appeared in 1894 as possible.

Others who provided invaluable support for this project are my parents, Donald and Maxine Duster, my brothers David and Daniel, as well as my uncle, Troy Duster, who has always been a huge advocate and cheerleader to my many ideas over the years. My friends Quentin Wyatt, Veronica Jenkins and Ernestine Yuille Weaver read drafts of the manuscript and gave me helpful suggestions for improvement.

My publisher, Benjamin Williams, and I worked very closely on every aspect of the book. He had some wonderful suggestions along the way and shared his vision, concepts and ideas with me. This truly has been a collaboration and I think the book is so much better than it would have been without his input.

My uncle, Benjamin C. Duster, has always insisted that I know my history. In addition, my aunt, Alfreda Duster Ferrell, and my cousin, Tiana Ferrell, have been a huge source of encouragement and enthusiasm over the years. There are dozens of other aunts, uncles, cousins, friends, fellow writers, book club members, classmates, neighbors, co-workers, committee members and teachers who helped me hone my skills and made sure that I kept striving to reach my goals.

How We're Related
to Ida B. Wells-Barnett

Ida B. Wells and Ferdinand L. Barnett
had four children:
Charles Aked, Herman, Ida and Alfreda

Children
Ferdinand and Ida's youngest daughter,
Alfreda Barnett, married Benjamin C. Duster
and had five children:
Benjamin, Charles, Donald, Alfreda, and Troy.

Grandchildren
*Benjamin C. Duster, Charles E. Duster, Donald L. Duster,
Alfreda Duster Ferrell and <u>Troy Duster</u>*
collectively had fifteen children.

Great-grandchildren
<u>*Michelle Duster*</u> is one of those fifteen
great-grandchildren.
She is the daughter of Donald L. Duster.

Charles E. Duster, Jr. is a researcher who earned his bachelor's degree in Economics from Northwestern University. A native Chicagoan, he is the son of Charles E. Duster, Sr. and a great-grandson of Ida B. Wells.

Troy Duster, Ph.D. is Silver Professor of Sociology and Director of the Institute for the History of the Production of Knowledge at New York University. He also holds an appointment as chancellor's professor at the University of California, Berkeley. He is the author of several books including *The Legislation of Morality* (The Free Press, 1970); *Cultural Perspectives on Biological Knowledge* (Ablex, 1984) with Karen Garrett; and *Backdoor to Eugenics* (Routledge, 2003 – 2nd ed). He has written numerous articles on youth unemployment and post-industrialism, diversity and higher education. A native Chicagoan, he is a grandson of Ida B. Wells.

158

Michelle Duster is a writer, speaker, project manager and artist. She earned a bachelor's degree in Psychology from Dartmouth College and a master's degree in Communications from the New School for Social Research. A native Chicagoan, she is a great-granddaughter of Ida B. Wells.

Ida

In Her Own Words

The timeless writings
of Ida B. Wells from 1893

African Americans were deliberately and systematically eliminated from participating in the preparation and exhibition of the Columbian Exposition (World's Fair) of 1893. The fact that an entire group of people who had been free citizens for almost thirty years, and who had made important contributions to the development of the nation were not given representation at such a significant international forum, provoked a protest.

A small group of four people contributed to a pamphlet entitled *The Reason Why the Colored American is not in the World's Columbian Exposition.* Thousands of pamphlets were distributed. *Class Legislation,* attributed to Ida B. Wells, and *Lynch Law,* written by Ida B. Wells, were two sections included in the pamphlet. The pieces give a glimpse for today's readers to understand the cruelty and hypocrisy of the country at that time.

ISBN: 978-0-9802398-1-2